Power

LEARNING CI... NHAM

Concepts in the Social Sciences

Series Editor: Frank Parkin

Published Titles

Concepts in the Social Sciences

Power

Keith Dowding

Open University Press
Buckingham

Open University Press
Celtic Court
22 Ballmoor
Buckingham
MK18 1XW

First Published 1996

A catalogue record of this book is available from the British Library

ISBN 0 335 19440 0 (pbk)   0 335 19441 9 (hbk)

Typeset by Type Study, Scarborough
Printed in Great Britain by J.W. Arrowsmith Limited, Bristol

Contents

I would like to dedicate this book to Richard Kimber and Jonathan Dancy who taught me at Keele University where I studied politics and philosophy as an undergraduate. Richard first introduced me to public choice, whose methods fascinated me but whose conclusions often appalled me. I soon learned that the devil only has the best tunes when he is playing the instruments. Richard encouraged and supported me enormously in my early career and gave me confidence in my own abilities. Jonathan Dancy encouraged me in another way by scaring the seven shades of . . . somnolency out of me, but in doing so, quite simply, taught me how to think.

Preface

This is the second book on power I have written. It takes much the same line as the first, though here I have concentrated less on criticizing others and more on explaining how we can understand power in society. It expands some of the themes of my earlier *Rational Choice and Political Power* and more directly suggests methods of studying power empirically. I hope it will be of interest both to philosophers concerned with the idea of power itself, and political scientists intending to study power in society.

There has long been a power debate in political science. It eventually ran out of steam, with both sides apparently thinking they had won. On one side were elitists, who felt that despite democratic structures power was largely in the hands of a small number of people based around senior political, bureaucratic and business interests. On the other were the pluralists, who through a series of case studies showed that at the very least different elites dominated in different issue areas and often the elites did not get all they wanted. There was power in the democratic system after all, not only through the ballot box but more especially through the pressure group process. Others argued that power was more diffuse, caught up with issues concerning the real freedoms and interests of people, freedoms and interests which go beyond those which most people recognize. The system of power was too complex to be studied with the simple empirical tools of the behavioural political scientist. This book suggests that we can study power empirically, but we have to understand how it operates, both causally through the actions of individuals, groups and organizations and through the incentives which lead people to behave in one way or another. People's actions and interests are structured by the set of relationships they have with one another and the world around them. We have to understand how these operate, by modelling them before we causally examine the operation of actors' power. When we model the power structure we find we need to introduce a separate concept – that of luck – which enables some to get what they want without trying. Luck is not power and it is the failure to understand luck that led much of the early debate astray. In this short account of power, I hope to show the reader how to model power relations in empirical research while understanding that a large part of the old community power debate was normative, based upon writers' expectations about how the world should operate, which entails views about how it could operate.

This book was written while I was engaged in a project looking at the power structure in London, funded by the Economic and Social Research Council grant number L311253008. I would like to thank my colleagues on that project, Patrick Dunleavy, Desmond King, Helen Margetts and Yvonne Rydin, for stimulating empirical research based upon new ways of understanding power. Our results will be contained in *Power in the Metropolis*, co-authored by the team and published by Cambridge University Press.

I would like to thank Brian Barry for correcting two errors in the original manuscript and for his general comments.

Keith Dowding
Oxford, 1996

1
Power To and Power Over

Why is power important?

Politics is about 'who gets what, when, how', wrote Harold Laswell in 1936. Individuals and groups get whatever they get because of what they and others do, because of the way society is structured, and because of the rules and conventions which govern the accepted way of doing things. To explain how someone obtains something, you need to study the causes of the outcomes which result from social activity. The causal story should also tell you why they got it when they did and also how they got it. Such causal stories are difficult to tell, and in political science we are more interested in the general features of society which explain why different groups get what they get. In telling the causal story of how a given individual or group achieved a desired outcome, we need to understand the nature of the rules and conventions under which people behave, and how those rules and conventions came into being. This gives an institutional focus. We also have to understand how society is structured and how that structure came into being. This gives a structural focus. Finally, we need to describe and explain the actual details of the relevant actors' behaviour. This gives a behavioural focus.

Telling such a story of politics is to tell a story about power in society. It tells us about the nature of the power structure, and it tells us about the power of actors themselves. Political power is important, because it constitutes the very fabric of politics and of society itself. The answers to questions about power in society are answers to questions about the very nature of politics and the policy process. One cannot study politics without an understanding of the nature of power. False views about power give partial views of politics and of society. It is for this reason that political power has been such a controversial topic in political science.

The post-war debate on the nature of political power and therefore the nature of the state and society has concerned three very different views. The elitists have generally argued that a few people dominate politics. They are powerful and govern largely in their own interests. There are several brands of elitism. Some believe that elites are largely based around personalities, families or social classes. Others see elites as holding certain social roles. For example, the state autonomists argue that the state, or at least state actors, has its own interests and only takes into account the views of other groups when these do not rival those of state actors.

This elite view of society was challenged by political scientists who concentrated upon the decision-making process itself and spent less time looking at the family and social backgrounds of key decision-makers. Pluralists argued that while it is true that a relatively small number of people hold key decision-making positions, those decision-makers are influenced by a great number of other people through the group process. Groups affect political decisions by bringing costs to key decision-makers, thus ensuring that the governing elites do not always get their own way.

This debate was highly charged, for normatively it makes a great deal of difference to the health of a democracy whether a few or many people affect the key decisions in communities within the nation. However, the debate itself was more concerned with trying accurately to describe and explain the nature of the decision-making process and the nature of the structures of power in the USA and other countries. Each side used different approaches to studying power and, perhaps, used different concepts of power. The arguments between the two rival approaches and their sub-branches was methodological as much as substantive, normative as much as empirical. A third group of writers has come to see power as an essentially contested and largely unempirical phenomenon. For these writers there is little point in trying to study power empirically or to judge between rival views of the power structure.

By re-examining the nature of power, and demarcating power from 'luck', we shall be able to understand how we can empirically study power and see what the empirical differences are between the rival accounts of the power structure. We can understand how the rival methodologies can be used in conjunction with each other in a consistent and coherent manner. We shall see that this conception of power can be used at the personal as well as the state level. Power is based upon resources, but it is not the same as resources. We can see how it is that some groups may be privileged and yet not powerful themselves, or be powerful and gain through the operation of the power structure without themselves wielding power. We can come to see the truths in the pluralist account of society, yet see how elites and business often do dominate, not only through their power but also because of luck.

Power and cause

Power and cause are intimately related. Indeed, some of the earliest analyses of causation (Berkeley 1962: sect. 60, p. 94; Hume 1975: sect. 10, part 2, pp. 32–40) used the concept of our power to make things happen as a metaphor to help explain the nature of causation in the natural world. To decide to move one's arm to throw a ball shows the conjunction of 'decision to move arm', 'the moving of the arm' and the 'moving of the ball'. It may be thought that the decision causes the arm to move, and the arm moving causes the ball to move. When we see one ball moving and hitting another ball, we expect the second ball to move in response to the collision with the first. The direction in which the second ball moves, and how far, depends upon the speed and mass of each ball and the angle of the strike. Seeing these events occurring many times leads us to see in the world the constant conjunction of cause and effect, just as we experience the constant conjunction of our power to do things and its results. Ironically, given the original use of individual power as a way of explaining causation, some modern writers have used causation in order to explain power (Simon 1969; Nagel 1975), while others have substituted cause for power (Dahl 1968: 410). However, causation and power are not the same.

Power is a dispositional concept. To say that I have the power to throw a stone 50 metres is to say that I *could* throw that stone 50 metres, not that I *am* throwing it that far. It is to say that I have the capacity to throw it. The capacity of an object, in this case myself, is a dispositional property of that object. Dispositional properties are more difficult to study than non-dispositional ones, such as the colour of my eyes. If you want to know the colour of my eyes you just have to look at them: they exist in the actual world. If you want to know how far I can throw a stone, you cannot simply watch me throw one, because when you see me do so I may not be trying very hard and only manage to send it a few metres. Or I may never throw a stone in my entire life. Either way, I may still have the capacity to throw a stone 50 metres. In these cases my capacity to throw exists in the actual world, but my throwing a stone 50 metres only occurs in a possible one. Dispositional properties are essentially 'counter-actual'; that is, they refer to what might be and not necessarily to what is.[1] Nicholas Rescher (1975: 132) says they 'have one foot in the realm of the actual, another in that of the possible'. The problem for studying power is that we may have to discover the power of actors without actually seeing them wield that power. This is partly because they do not always use all their power, and partly because, even when they do, the nature of the political process and the social world means that some actors may try to exercise that power away from the prying eyes of those trying to study them. Dispositional properties are theoretical in character, and we have to approach power in society theoretically, though we shall want to corroborate our hypothesis empirically whenever we can.

Two concepts of power

There are two concepts of power: 'power to' and 'power over'. It does not make much sense to say 'actor A has power'; we have to say what actor A has the power to do. 'Power to' can therefore be thought of as the most basic use of the term 'power'. Many writers, however, do not see this as the important aspect of power in political contexts. Rather, they see the power of one actor over another as the important use of political power. Now 'power over' implies 'power to', for A will have power over B to make B do x. A has the power to make B do x. 'Power to' and 'power over' may be described as 'outcome power' and 'social power' respectively, the first because it is the power to bring about outcomes, the second because it necessarily involves a social relation between at least two actors (Dowding 1991: 48). We may give a formal definition of these two concepts:

outcome power = the ability of an actor to bring about or help to bring about outcomes

social power = the ability of an actor deliberately to change the incentive structure of another actor or actors to bring about or help to bring about outcomes

The first definition is straightforward, whereas the second requires some explanation. Having power over others is a complex relationship. Getting some outcome x by using others to make it happen may transpire in blatant or subtle ways. We can capture this range by writing of 'incentive structures'. The incentive structure facing an actor is the full set of costs and benefits of behaving in one way rather than another. Typically actors have power over others to the extent that they can manipulate others' incentive structure. Taking away options from a choice set, or making the costs of an action higher or lower, or making the benefits higher or lower [or making the costs and benefits appear to have changed (Dowding 1992)], will encourage some actions and discourage others. Changing the incentive structure may involve straightforward coercion, or more subtle alterations in the incentives to behave one way or another. The Conservative central government in Britain altered the incentive structure of many actors during its long tenure of power. It brought about radical changes in the regulation of finance and industry, trades unions, the relationship between central and local government, and in many other areas.

We may give a simple example of how one group of actors chose to behave differently because of the way central government changed their incentive structure. In 1991, the left-wing Labour council in the inner London borough of Lambeth applied for money under the City Challenge Project to set up Brixton Challenge. This is a private corporation largely supported by central government funds. Its role is to encourage business to develop in Brixton, which is located within the jurisdiction of Lambeth Council. Brixton Challenge tries to encourage development by working with local business, the local council, housing associations and other bodies in order to generate redevelopment and provide jobs in an area of high unemployment and with many social problems. The ruling Labour council in Lambeth was not keen on the City Challenge idea. The councillors believed that it was better to have an integrated plan for the whole of Lambeth, rather than just one area. They were not keen on the public–private partnerships necessary under the City

Challenge concept, preferring for example to keep housing policy in the public sector, rather than involve housing associations and private landlords. Nevertheless, despite their ideological objections to the Conservative government's policy, they bid for and received City Challenge money. Why? Quite simply the incentives set up by the Conservative government made it irrational for Lambeth to do otherwise.[2]

Most local government funding in Britain comes from central government. The City Challenge money was taken from money that would otherwise go to local councils as a normal part of the central grant. Those areas which received money from the City Challenge project would be advantaged over ones which did not. Councils which did not have a successful City Challenge bid would therefore lose out. The Labour councillors of Lambeth still chose of their own free will to bid for City Challenge money. But they did so because the environment in which they made their decisions had been changed by the policy of the Conservative central government.

Changing others' incentive structures may be pernicious or beneficial. We may do it to bring about what we desire, and this may be in others' interests or against them. We may change others' incentive structures in ways which reduce the scope of their reasonably possible actions, or in ways which enable them to do things that previously seemed impossible. Education changes people's incentives to behave in one way rather than another by leading them to understand the world around them in new ways. A housebound person may be enabled to get out by means of financial assistance or products which allow her to live a life closer to that of the more abled. Welfare payments generally change people's incentive structures. Those on the right suggest that too high welfare encourages indolence; those on the left, on the contrary, suggest it enables people to overcome stricken circumstances and play a fuller part in society. Either way, welfare changes incentive structures.

The definition of social power involves the word 'deliberate'. This is important for both analytic and normative reasons. If the word 'deliberate' were not used in relation to social power, the two sorts of power would collapse into one whenever one actor's outcome power affected others. On the whole, whenever we act we change others' incentive structures. The sum of all market transactions determines the price of goods and thus my entering into one product market rather than another affects your incentives to buy one sort of

product or another. Sometimes this may affect you significantly –
for example, when I put in an offer on a house that you are
interested in purchasing – but the effect on price of my purchasing,
say, a certain brand of toothpaste is negligible. Nevertheless, our
actions do affect others around us. The two definitions of social
and outcome power are separate, however, for under outcome
power some result occurs because some actor desires it and the
effect upon others is a by-product and irrelevant to the actor's
scheme. Under social power the choice situation of others is
changed in order to bring about some outcome. Thus the Conservative government wanted to ensure that local authorities
would bring businessmen into important planning positions
through their occupying positions on the boards of City Challenge
Corporations. It was satisfied that many Conservative authorities
would do so, but through setting up the incentives correctly they
were able to involve left-wing Labour councils as well. More
directly, they forced councils to open up contracts to competitive
tendering by making it illegal not to do so.

We shall see that while the two parts of the definition of political
power are analytically distinct – that is, they are usefully dis-
tinguished for the purposes of analysis – often they may be hard to
separate ontologically. The analytic distinction is useful for the
purposes of analysis, for it suggests a two-fold strategy. First, study
the actors' *choice situation*: examine the situation as it exists and
see what rational strategies should be adopted for actors to achieve
their aims. This involves two stages: (1) imagine a parametric
environment, one in which a group of people faces problems even
though there is no opposition to their plans; (2) assume the group
faces a strategic situation where other groups desire different
outcomes. We shall see how we can approach this task in Chapter
3, where we look at models of bargaining and collective action and
suggest a method for studying power in society. The second aspect
of power suggests that we may study the development of actors'
choice situations. How did they come to be facing this set of
incentives? Was this situation engendered by the deliberate actions of others, or did it occur through some non-deliberative
process akin to natural selection?

The first stage is ahistorical, the second involves a closer look at
the history. Sometimes we may be more interested in the ahistorical questions, sometimes in the historical ones. Both are

required for a fully rounded picture of the existing power structures in society.

Two types of game

'Power to' may involve cooperation; 'power over' seems to involve conflict. By working together people can achieve far more than if they work alone. By cooperating people gain in power. Weber (1978: 1399) suggests that all politics involves conflict. For this reason, most people see 'power over' as the most important aspect of political power. However, some form of conflict may underlie even the most cooperative situations. We may agree that certain outcomes are desirable and may even agree that it requires the cooperation of many people to bring about those outcomes. It does not follow that we will immediately agree to cooperate. This problem is known as the collective action problem (Olson 1971; Hardin 1982; Sandler 1992; see Chapter 2), and it may be modelled by the use of game theory.[3]

The theory of games models interdependent actions, that is, when the actions of two or more people (or collective actors such as firms or government agencies) jointly determine some outcome. The choices of these actors are shaped by the social environment in which they find themselves, which includes the nature of the interrelationship of players of the game. In fact, the type of game that the players are engaged upon may be said to constitute their incentive structure. Game theory provides a way of formalizing social structures and examining the effects of those structures upon individuals' decisions. It therefore provides an ideal way of examining the structure of power in a society.

In this book, we shall use some simple games to illustrate the nature of power in society in a manner which transcends some rather sterile old debates in the history of political science. We begin here by looking at the difference between two different sorts of game: constant-sum (or zero-sum) games and variable-sum games. The former are examples of straightforward conflict, the latter of potential cooperation. Consider the two matrices in Figure 1.1.

In each game-matrix in Figure 1.1 there are two actors. Each has a choice of two actions. Players 1 and 3 can either do A or B; Players 2 and 4 can either do X or Y. Associated with each set of actions

		(a) Pure conflict Player 2				(b) Pure coordination Player 4	
		X	Y			X	Y
Player	A	2,3	4,1	Player	A	1,1	2,3
1	B	1,4	3,2	3	B	3,2	4,4

Figure 1.1   Games of pure conflict and pure coordination.

(A,X; A,Y; B,X; B,Y) is a set of 'payoffs' for each player. The numbers in the matrices represent the payoffs: the first number represents the payoff to Player 1 in 1.1(a) and to Player 3 in 1.1(b), the second number to Player 2 in 1.1(a) and to Player 4 in 1.1(b). Thus in Figure 1.1(a), if Player 1 does A and Player 2 does X, the first gets a payoff of 2 and the second a payoff of 3.

Figure 1.1(a) is a constant-sum game and represents pure conflict. It is called a constant-sum game because the numbers associated with each pair of actions sum to a constant amount; in this example, they add up to 5. It can represent pure conflict, since one player's gain is another player's loss, and the strategy adopted by each player is dependent upon the other's actions. So if Player 1 does A, Player 2 will want to do X, thus ensuring a payoff of 3 to herself with a payoff of 2 to Player 1. If Player 1 were to choose B, then Player 2 would again choose X, thus ensuring a payoff of 4 for herself but a payoff of only 1 to Player 1. If the players play in that order, then the rational strategy is for the first player, Player 1, to choose A, thus ensuring a payoff of 2. If he chose B, he would end up with only 1. If Player 2 were to go first, he would choose X to ensure a payoff of at least 3. Again Player 1 would choose A in order to receive a payoff of 2 rather than 1. It is easy to see that if the players make their moves simultaneously, the same outcome (A,X) will result. Here we can ascertain simply by consulting the matrix that in terms of the payoff scores, Player 1 will do worse than Player 2. It is simply his bad luck to find himself in a game with a matrix drawn this way.

Figure 1.1(b) shows a variable-sum game of pure cooperation or coordination. The payoffs associated with each pair of actions vary from 2 (A,X) to 5 (A,Y; B,X) to 8 (B,Y). Here we should expect both players to choose to reach their highest payoffs, Player 3 choosing B and Player 4 choosing Y. The only difficulty that real players might have in playing these games to the predicted outcomes is if they were unaware of the payoff structures to themselves and others. Note, though, in both games, that if both players knew only their own payoff structure, each would still choose the same way.

In these two games, the players can each achieve payoffs of between 1 and 4. In a counteractual sense, all four can achieve the same payoff as each other. Given completely free will and genuine choice, either player could choose either possible course of action. However, the structure of the games strongly suggests a different outcome. In Figure 1.1(b), the players jointly have the power to each gain their highest payoff. In Figure 1.1(a), they cannot both achieve the highest payoff, and whereas Player 2 is lucky enough to ensure that she either gets her third highest or her highest payoff, Player 1 can only assure himself of his second worst payoff. The power of each player thus varies. Each can avoid their worst outcome, but they vary in their ability to achieve better outcomes. These matrices thus illustrate two important lessons about the nature of power. First, the power of individuals can be enhanced through cooperative actions when it is to the advantage of people to cooperate. Secondly, the power of individuals varies with the nature of the circumstances in which they find themselves. How those circumstances arise is important to those interested in considering the social justness of unequal power. For the time being, I will regard the position of actors in social situations as their luck. Players 3 and 4 are just lucky that they can achieve their optimal payoffs because the structure of their interests is coincidental. Players 1 and 2 are less lucky for their game is one of conflict, but Player 1 is the unluckiest of them all for he can only ensure his second worst payoff. At least he does not get the worst payoff.

We should note one final aspect of the interpretation of these games. The numbers can be taken to represent the utility associated with each payoff. All four players wish to maximize their own utility. Utility here is not the same as self-interest, though game theorists usually (even if only implicitly) assume so. I will assume that people are on the whole self-interested, but not exclusively so; they do take into account the interests of their close associates, friends, family, work colleagues, even of the wider society and environment. Assuming self-interest generally allows us to simplify our understandings of the social world and is a reasonable assumption to explain mass behaviour directed at a given target, though it is not a reasonable assumption to make about all the actions of any given individual.

Games of conflict and cooperation

Game theorists have traditionally maintained a distinction between cooperative and non-cooperative game theory. This distinction does not have anything to do with whether cooperation may result or not, but indicates whether or not it is possible for the players to make binding agreements. This distinction is beginning to disappear, since the nature of binding agreements in cooperative game theory may be analysed through non-cooperative game-theoretic models. I want to make a different distinction here: between games where cooperation seems to have no role – such as in Figure 1.1(a) – those where cooperation is structurally suggested by the nature of the game – such as in Figure 1.1(b) – and those where cooperation brings benefits but where conflict also exists. The last games may be described as games of both conflict and cooperation. It is these which have proved most interesting to game theorists. The following three games have each been extensively analysed in the literature and have been given names associated with stories that may explain the payoffs.

Figure 1.2 represents a coordination game with certain conflictual elements. (It may be seen as the basic script for most Hollywood love stories.) Each person wishes to go out for the evening with the other, but they have a different preference ordering about where they want to go. She wants to go to a rock concert, but he wants to go to the ballet. The way the 'Battle of the Sexes' works in most love stories is that the two lovers both want to spend their lives together, but have different preferences over how those lives are to be run. Neither wants to compromise on an important aspect of their lives,

		Him	
		Rock	Ballet
Her	Rock	4,3	2,1
	Ballet	1,2	3,4

Figure 1.2   Battle of the Sexes.

their career, their other friends, where they are to live and so on. Since in this game both individuals generally share an interest in coordinating either on (Rock,Rock) or (Ballet,Ballet), we should expect one of these outcomes. But in the negotiations to this end, or over a series of games with this basic structure (called an iterated Battle of the Sexes), both parties may represent themselves differently. They may try to reach a series of compromises, so that sometimes he gets his first preference and sometimes she does. But the nature of the joint compromises may not be equal. He may prove to be the stronger personality and get his way more often. One of the tactics he might adopt to this end is to pretend that he is less interested in spending the evening with her than he really is, and that he is less interested in her than she is in him. He demonstrates enough interest in the woman to ensure that she remains interested in him but pretends that he is at least as interested in the ballet in order not only to 'win the girl' but also to win her on his terms. If she does not act similarly, then she will be the one who is continually compromising, and the film – and indeed life – would not be so interesting.

In such a battle, each will develop a reputation based upon how they play the game. If he proves unwilling ever to go to her favourite places, then his reputation will develop as a tough, uncompromising individual, not a particularly loving person. If she compromises too often, then she will get the reputation of a 'doormat' – someone others can wipe their feet on. Reputations may develop without either party particularly wanting them: she does not want to be a doormat, nor he someone who is unloving. If they are not careful they may become their reputations. But reputations may also be engendered deliberately. He may try to act uncompromisingly, yet be terrified of not dating her; he just pretends his payoff structure is different from what it really is for his own advantage. This game can teach us two important aspects about power in society. First, not only are one's own preferences important in getting what one wants, but equally important is how others perceive those preferences. Secondly, reputation is a key resource. The importance of reputation can be seen by considering another favourite game-theoretic model.

The game in Figure 1.3 is called 'Chicken', after the game played by youths driving cars at each other along a roadway. You either swerve or not. If neither does, then disaster ensues as both cars

Player 2

		X	Y
Player	A	3,3	2,4
1	B	4,2	1,1

Figure 1.3 Chicken.

Player 2

		X	Y
Player	A	1000000,1000000	999000,1000001
1	B	1000001,999000	0, 0

Figure 1.4 Chicken game of high risk loss.

Player 2

		X	Y
Player	A	3,3	2,4
1	B	101,2	1,1

Figure 1.5 Non-symmetrical Chicken game.

collide head-on. If both swerve, then both lose honour; but if one swerves, then he is 'chicken' and the other is the winner. This is a game in which reputation counts for all when iterated. It is hard to tell what each player should do in this game by simply studying the matrix. There is no 'rational' strategy. The risky strategy is B for Player 1 and Y for Player 2, promising the rewards of 4 if the other plays contrarily. How great a risk one should take depends on the circumstances of the battle, the nature of one's preference and the exact nature of the payoff structure. In Figure 1.3, we have represented the payoffs as lying between 1 and 4. However, consider the payoff structure in the Chicken games depicted in Figures 1.4 and 1.5.

In Figure 1.4, the risky strategy may seem too risky, as the costs of failure are so high. Both players may be expected to play their non-risky strategy, A for Player 1 and X for Player 2, though disaster is still possible if both players calculate that the other will not take the risk simply because the risks are so high. If the payoffs are not symmetrical, as in Figure 1.5, then we can expect Player 1 to play B and Player 2 to play X or Y, at least partly dependent upon whether or not she knows what the first player's payoffs are. How bad is the worst payoff? If it is death, then perhaps one will not take the risk; if it is a damaged fender on a stolen car, then perhaps one might. The key to this game is trying to understand what your opponent is doing, and what signals you give to her.

It may appear strange to suggest that this game, which, from the story that gives it its name, seems to be one of pure conflict, is a game of both conflict and cooperation. However, by inspecting the matrix, one can see that (A,X) brings both players their second highest payoff. Chicken games can represent the possibilities of collective action for genuine benefits, where the dangers of not helping may lead to disaster. Environmental problems can be seen as Chicken games. If each nation builds supertrawlers that scour the world's oceans for fish, over-fishing will result, fish stocks will diminish, and then no-one can fish. If we create quotas that ensure fish stocks do not dwindle, then everyone can continue to fish. If some parties cheat on the quotas, then they gain an advantage by being able to take more than their share. If too many cheat, then the fish stocks decrease, though the world's oceans may be able to support a few cheaters as long as most stick to their quotas. Some nations may try to establish a situation where they are accepted as cheats, as Japan and Norway managed for many years with regard to whaling. But there are dangers in trying to create a reputation for toughness (Ward 1987a, 1989).

In a more mundane but equally important way, Chicken can represent the power relations that exist in the household. Two individuals may each want a clean house but prefer that the other does the cleaning. Each may refuse to clean, pretending that they are less concerned about the mess than they really are. The one whose preferences for a clean house are strongest, or who has the weakest will in the psychological battle, may lose out. If it becomes expected by society that one type of person will usually clean, then people in that group may find the social pressures greatest. Or they may find that people of that type (or gender!) are expected to have the type of personality which succumbs. Strong-willed women may then be less likely to find partners and breed, and natural selection, based upon social or institutional forces, will lead to one gender having different characteristics than the other. Individual women may then find it harder to resist the pressures when locked in a

Player 2

		X	Y
Player	A	3,3	1,4
1	B	4,1	2,2

Figure 1.6   Prisoners' Dilemma.

Chicken game with a man. Such a model may stand as a motif for gender relations in the household (Carling 1991).

Chicken is a game which demonstrates the complexity of individual decision-making when there are benefits from cooperation but also from a refusal to cooperate. It illustrates the advantages of free-riding upon the efforts of others. It shows that there are advantages to be gained through hiding one's preferences and developing a reputation. There are gains to be had through building a reputation for toughness because one may be able to free-ride more easily upon the efforts of others. Game theory can also teach us that there are benefits of gaining a reputation for being willing to cooperate. Trustworthiness and reliability are key aspects of many cooperative relationships which develop over time as the players continually interact with one another.

One of the game theorists' favourite games over the years has been the Prisoners' Dilemma. When iterated it demonstrates how important a reputation for reliability can be. In its non-iterated form, it illustrates a paradox of rationality, showing how rational action may lead to a worse outcome than irrational action.

The Prisoners' Dilemma takes its name from a story where two people are arrested for a crime for which the police do not have the evidence to convict. But they do have enough evidence to convict on a lesser charge. Each criminal is offered the chance to confess to the bigger crime and receive leniency for himself while his partner goes to jail. If both confess, both go to jail, though with reduced sentences; if both keep quiet, then both get convicted on the lesser charge only. In Figure 1.6, Player 1 may choose to confess by playing B, or not confess by playing A. Player 2 similarly confesses when choosing Y and does not confess when choosing X.

Player 1 has the *dominant* strategy of B, *for no matter what Player 2 does*, Player 1 is better off playing B. If Player 2 plays X, then Player 1 gets 4 rather than the 3 he would have got playing A, and if

Player 2 plays Y, then Player 1 gets 2 rather than the 1 he would have got playing A. The matrix is symmetrical, so the same situation faces Player 2. She has the dominant strategy of Y. It would seem that in a non-repeated Prisoners' Dilemma, both players have a dominant rational strategy which leads to their third preferred payoff, whereas had they both played the irrational dominated strategy, they would each have got their second most preferred payoff. Universal cooperation is universally preferred to universal cheating, but universal cooperation is individually unstable (it is dominated and the players cannot make binding agreements) and individually inaccessible (it requires the cooperation of the other).

The result of the non-repeated Prisoners' Dilemma played by rational players is unchallengeable. Many have tried but the intuition that somehow the prisoners will manage to cooperate is based upon the fact that in real life people interact over and over again. In iterated Prisoners' Dilemmas, cooperation may result (Axelrod 1984). But it need not. The 'folk theorem' demonstrates that any finite pattern of cooperation or non-cooperation in an infinitely repeated Prisoners' Dilemma (and similar games) is possible (Rasmusen 1989: 92–4). Thus any intuition over the possibilities of cooperation or not in a repeated game like the Prisoners' Dilemma can be justified. It demonstrates that despite the benefits that collective action might bring, it may not always occur. As we shall see in Chapter 2, the collective action problem is only a problem not an impossibility.

The blame fallacy

We can see that with the problems of collective action that can be modelled, individuals may find difficulties in working together to promote common interests. Groups may fail to achieve their aims without there being any other group deliberately acting to stop them. To think that the powerlessness of people entails that there are other powerful people stopping them is an example of the blame fallacy. The blame fallacy asserts that because something did not turn out as intended, someone must be to blame. We can see this fallacy being asserted whenever there is some disaster, whether natural or human. Sometimes the burden of responsibility for a catastrophe may lie with individuals, sometimes not; but there will always be an effort to lay blame at someone's door. Many scholars have committed the blame fallacy while studying power in communities (Dowding 1991).

Power and game theory

Game theory is a theory of strategic interaction. It can teach us what are the best (and worst) strategies for responding to others in various different types of situations. Game theory can aid us in the process of understanding how actors react to one another's strategies. It can help us to understand why actors do not always work together to increase their overall outcome power. And it can help us to learn why different outcomes occur in similar circumstances. If we see games as representing the structures of society, we can learn how it is that different sets of individuals take on different sets of interests. Consider each of the matrices in Figures 1.1–1.6. With the exception of Figures 1.4 and 1.5, what defines the difference between the matrices is the relationship of the preferences of the two actors. The matrices define the structural relationship between the two players. The difference in the analysis, therefore, is a structural difference.

Game-theoretic explanation using such matrices is structural. We can also see from the matrices in Figures 1.4 and 1.5 that the cardinal preferences of the individuals affect what we might expect of their behaviour. So in order to understand power in society, we need to understand both the preferences – or more broadly the interests – of individuals and groups in society and the relationship between those actors. We need both individualist and structural explanation. This issue is taken up in the next chapter.

Notes

1 I prefer the term 'counteractual' to the more usual 'counterfactual', since it is odd to call facts 'counterfacts'. If I poke you in the eye it will hurt. And that's a fact.
2 Lambeth's ruling councillors had been behaving irrationally as a group for a long time during the 1980s. Politically divided, the ruling council was never sure if it was trying to govern Lambeth in the interests of the people given the constraints placed on it by central government, or whether it should wage full-scale war against the government using citizens as weapons in the ideological battle. By 1991, it was clear that the war was lost, and so too would the local Labour Party lose in municipal

elections unless they started to work with the new rules rather than against them.

3 There are now many good introductory books on game theory. The reader is advised to start with one of Steven Brams's (1990, 1994) books. Fudenberg and Tirole (1991) and Heap and Varoufakis (1995) are both good introductions which contain most of the important advances of recent years. Ordeshook (1986, 1992) and Morrow (1994) apply game theory more directly in political contexts.

2

Structure and
Interests

In the game-theoretic models considered in Chapter 1, we assumed that two individuals each have a set of preferences and are engaged in a 'game' defined in terms of the relationship of their preference orderings. It should be noted that all we know of the individuals are their preference orderings and their relationship one to another. The game is thus a description of the structure in which each individual finds him or herself. The expected result occurs because rational individuals, knowing their own preference ordering and the structure of the game, will play to achieve the best payoff given these circumstances. In this sense, game-theoretic explanation is structural. It is also individualistic: the payoffs occur because of the actions of the individuals and not because of some other cause. They act according to their 'situational logic' (Popper 1957: 147–52).

The game-theoretic models become interesting when they are applied to real situations which they resemble. But real people have a set of interests which go beyond a simple preference ordering. For one thing, real individuals play a whole host of games simultaneously with different people. The situations in which they find themselves are more complex and the structure of each game they play is not so obvious. They make mistakes which may lead someone analysing their behaviour to believe that their preferences are different from what they genuinely are. Furthermore, and importantly, real people do not come to the games they play in life with a simple preference ordering. Preferences and interests develop in us as we play the game of life.

To some extent, the very interactions we engage in create our preferences. Think once more of the Battle of the Sexes game. We saw that it could be in the strategic interest of the woman to pretend her preferences for spending the evening with the man are not as strong as they 'really' are, in order to try to force him to spend the evening at the rock concert. Similarly, he can pretend that his interest in her is not so strong and that he would rather go to the ballet on his own. These signals that each sends to the other create information that will lead to each assessing the worth of the other. He may begin to reassess his true desire to spend time with her, given that she seems intent on going to rock concerts rather than spending the evening with him. She may reassess her attitude towards a man who likes to go to the ballet. The very fact that each sends 'false' signals to the other may change the preferences of the other. They may decide that perhaps they are not suited to each other after all. We can ask, if each has sent 'false' signals, then are they wrong to think that they are not meant for each other?

Perhaps would-be lovers often regret their actions, and perhaps later fondly discuss together what might have been. But to claim that they were 'wrong' to decide they were not meant to be together would be to privilege the preferences given in Figure 1.2, rather than the preferences created through their interactions. Why should we privilege the preferences of Figure 1.2? In the game, they are simply assumed; in real life, these preferences are created through previous interactions. If he wanted initially to spend the evening with her on account of her gorgeous brown hair, and she with him because of his sexy smile, then surely the information that each had completely different tastes in entertainment can hardly be described as irrelevant. More particularly, if they both wanted to spend the evening together because each felt that the other had at earlier stages in the relationship demonstrated a strong desire to do so – 'you are interested in me, so I am interested in you' – then starting to play strategically at least demonstrates that each does not think the world of the other. For each has other preferences which they want to try to keep alive. Thus the initial preferences for each other are modified in the light of the strategic interactions which occur. So-called signalling games thus create new sets of preferences in the players, and we have no reason to suggest that any stage in the game is privileged and constitutes the 'real' preferences of the players. All we can say is that hiding their real preferences as they exist at any stage may cause them to develop preferences at a later

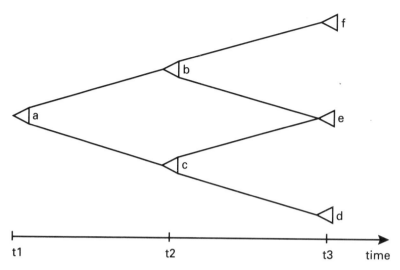

Figure 2.1   Path-dependency.

stage different from what they would have been had their true preferences been apparent at that earlier stage. Others' reactions to them were based on the 'false' preferences revealed, thus changing the course of the game.

Objective interests

This account of preference creation allows us to see how individuals may develop different sorts of preference at different stages of their life as a result of their behaviour in the past. And there may be no going back. A decision I have taken in the past may now create preferences in me that I cannot change for the preferences I might otherwise have developed. Preferences may thus be (at least partially) path-dependent.

Figure 2.1 suggests how, at each decision node, a path is chosen. Where one may get to from each decision node is partially dependent upon how one got to that node. Thus from *b* it is possible to get to *e* or *f*; whereas from *c* it is possible to get to *e* (or *d*) but not *f*. This point is developed below, but first I want to create a distinction between preferences and interests. 'Interest' usually finds expression in economic or quasi-economic discourse (Barry and Rae

1975: 382), but more importantly one's interests are dependent upon factors other than one's preferences. Interest is also dependent upon need, and need is a modal term that requires explanation in terms of something else. I may simply proclaim a preference for strawberries over raspberries, but if I proclaim a need for strawberries, then the question 'what for?' may be asked. A need thus denotes a requirement relating one's desires to one's present situation, but one may not realize what is necessary in order to bring about that desire. Thus preferences may create needs of which one is unaware.

Another important difference between desires and needs arises through the intensionality of the mental. What we desire is always some object under a description. If an individual needs something under a particular description, it does not follow that he needs a particular object, just one that falls under that description. However, while one may desire something under one description but not under another, one cannot need something under one description but not under another:

> To want to kill the man blocking your escape does not [entail] wanting to kill your own son, even though it is your son who is blocking your escape. What one needs, on the other hand, one needs whatever its description. If in order to escape, one needs to kill the man blocking one's way and the man is one's own son, then one needs to kill one's own son. (White 1975: 112)

While I may have my own subjective reasons for desiring something, I cannot have my own reasons for needing something. Those reasons are objective. However, the way we value something depends upon the way we understand it: we value it under some descriptions but not others (Schick 1982; Dowding 1992). Any set of desires entails a set of needs which hold whether or not the person who has the desires actually knows or understands her needs. Thus, as our desires change, so do our needs. The process of forming preferences itself creates needs which we may not understand, or may deny when they are pointed out. Many individuals hold inconsistent desires, but when the inconsistency is pointed out, rational individuals feel the need to drive out some in order to form a consistent set.

What do we mean when we talk about an individual's best interests? We could mean the highest items in someone's preference ordering. However, a game like the simple Prisoners' Dilemma demonstrates that individuals will not necessarily act to attain the outcome which is highest in their preference ordering. Given that preference orderings only make sense within the constraints under which individuals make choices, there is a problem with making sense of the idea of individual objective interests. The concept of individual subjective interests given a preference ordering subject to constraints can only mean the item which is the highest in the ordering. But this is not what we mean when we talk about someone's best interests.

Consider the ordering for one of the players in the Prisoners' Dilemma depicted in Figure 1.6. She orders the preferences $\{4 > 3 > 2 > 1\}$. Her first preference is 4. Is this in her best interests? In a sense it is, for it is the outcome she most prefers of those on offer. Yet we know that given the structure of the simple Prisoners' Dilemma she cannot obtain her most preferred outcome, and any attempt to do so will leave her with her third most preferred outcome. That choice then is not in her best interests or, rather, being in the situation of having to make that choice is not in her best interests. In other words, it is not in your own best interests to be faced with the decision structure called 'Prisoners' Dilemma'. Can we say that this notion of best interests is also merely a preference, but one even higher in the ordering? In other words, she has an ordering $\{5 > 4 > 3 > 2 > 1\}$, where 5 = not face a decision within a 'Prisoners' Dilemma' game. This seems to equate best interests with highest preference. However, this cannot be correct because preference orderings are the order in which individuals place alternatives given constraints and, by hypothesis, the constraint in this example is that the player faces the decision situation called 'Prisoners' Dilemma'. In other words, alternative 5 does not enter into the preference ordering. This may be one way we can distinguish best interests from mere preferences. Individual interests are constituted by the conditions under which individuals would like to be able to choose from the alternatives under offer. Thus an individual's best interest is being able to choose his first preference (4 in the matrix), rather than having to choose a strategy (a line in the matrix): B for Player 1 and Y for Player 2. The players' best interests are unbounded by the actual constraints under which choice is made; their preferences are bounded by the choice constraints.

This may be extended by distinguishing between objective interests based on needs and subjective desires. Thus the argument that choosing the 4 outcome rather than the B or Y line is in the players' best interests requires also the recognition that certain conditions must be satisfied for that alternative to be open to them. These conditions require going outside the Prisoners' Dilemma structure. Of course, if those conditions are not naturally attainable, then the needs cannot be met and the interest vanishes, for one cannot be held to have interests which cannot exist.

More complex calculations can be made. For example, while players prefer 4 to 3, they also prefer 3 to 2. The conditions for individually attaining 4 may be too difficult; the players cannot step outside the Prisoners' Dilemma. Option 4 thus becomes practically (though not logically) unattainable. If so, then 3 may be recognized as being in each individual's best interests. The requirements for attaining 3 may involve changing the choice structure for each individual from that of the simple Prisoners' Dilemma into something which makes option 3 available for all and which may be in each individual's interest. Here, then, we have attained a divergence between preferences and interests. That is, 4 is the player's most-preferred alternative, but 3 is in her best interests for only 3 is (practically) attainable, once the constraints under which choice is made are altered by the collective actions of the individuals whose preference orderings we are considering. Such a shift empowers individuals; it allows them to attain some outcomes more easily. Changing the choice situation of people is thus an important way of altering their individual and collective power.

Preference formation

We may further illustrate the difference between preferences and interests by considering the different ways in which people form preferences and gain interests. Dunleavy (1991) makes an ostensive categorical distinction between 'endogenous' and 'exogenous' interests. Endogenous interests are ones we just have. We like strawberries and therefore have an interest in ensuring that strawberry producers are able to make a profit. Our endogenous interests we have simply by virtue of our personal characteristics (however those are developed; see below). An exogenous interest is one which we have by virtue of the circumstances in which we find ourselves. Thus someone in the trucking industry has an interest in government policies towards haulage firms. Someone working at McDonald's has an interest in the government's policy towards the regulation of casual labour. Quite what those interests are may depend upon other personal circumstances. A lorry driver may desire regulation of the haulage business if he is an employee of a large profitable firm, or may oppose regulation if he is self-employed or works for a small firm that may go under if regulations are tightened. Someone may desire greater regulation of casual labour in order to improve their own working conditions if they foresee a lifetime of only casual work; a law student working at McDonald's to pay for law school may oppose regulation if it makes it less likely that she will be employed in preference to someone otherwise unemployed. What is important in these examples is that the McDonald's worker has an interest in regulation as it applies to McDonald's, and the trucker as it applies to the haulage business. Their interest in regulation – perhaps the same bill – is dependent upon the conditions in which they find themselves; it is exogenous. This suggests that exogenous interests are 'structurally suggested' by our circumstances.

The distinction between endogenous and exogenous interests was described as ostensive and categorical. It is ostensive – demonstrated by example – of two categories: interests we have because of who we are and interests we have because of the situation in which we find ourselves. But these are not natural categories and, as has been suggested above, we may become who we are because of the situations in which we find ourselves. For example, even simple preferences for food may hide a history of development deriving from the power or class structure of a society. Some people prefer the taste of white bread to that of brown bread and some prefer brown to white. However, one of the ways in which we develop a taste for one sort of bread rather than another is by eating bread of that sort over a period of time. You may prefer white to brown because that is what you were fed as a child. Until recently, white bread was thought to be superior to brown owing to nineteenth-century social snobbery (Tannahill 1975: 316). Now brown, unprocessed bread is thought to be better for you, and more people are eating brown bread. Similarly, many people eat branflakes for breakfast. Usually they begin to do so because they are told that they need roughage, and they develop a taste for them.

Yet branflakes provide far less effective roughage than fresh vegetables. Once it became known in the 1950s that roughage was important to diet, the major bread producers found in branflakes a profitable way of using the excess bran they had from the refining process necessary to produce white bread. Thus we can see that even for simple endogenous tastes, we can work in some sort of power relations. We can see that even for simple tastes a history can be told.

We need a strategy for understanding the interests of individuals and groups in society in order to start modelling their power relations in the manner I have suggested. I develop a three-part strategy based on three theses (Dowding 1991: 32–44).

The first, the *ontological* thesis, suggests that what is in one's interest is much more than what one merely desires, because interests are partially dependent upon needs. Individuals may be wrong about their own interests because they are unaware of the particular needs concomitant upon their desires. We can thus make sense of objective interests without entirely divorcing those interests from individuals' own deep-rooted desires.

The *epistemological* thesis suggests that while some interests are entirely dependent upon certain desires which may be said just to happen (i.e. they are endogenous to an individual), most interests are also dependent upon factors external to the individual (i.e. they are exogenous). If we can know an individual's endogenous desires, we may then be able to discover her interests in precisely the same way that the agent does for herself. Thus interests may be said to be 'objective' in a further sense; they are open to inspection by all and individuals do not have privileged access to their own interests.

The *methodological* thesis suggests that we can discover individuals' interests by studying their behaviour. But this behavioural method must include both a theory of action and knowledge of individuals' choice situation. Careful behaviouralism includes both a theory of action and analysis of individuals' choice situation. Armed with innocuous assumptions about individuals' desires and with analysis of the conditions under which choice is made, we can discover what individuals' interests are.

In order to study power in society, we need to follow the methodological thesis on interests in order to discover interests and then to see how far the structures of power in society work with individuals' interests and how far they work against them. We must bear this in mind when considering the blame fallacy, and not think that because some group's interests are being served this must be because they are powerful. They may simply be lucky. (The concept of luck is developed further in Chapters 3 and 4.)

It is important to understand when modelling society that we are examining the power structure; it does not follow that there is such a thing as 'structural power'. Some writers have tried to develop an account in which power is held by structures in society. It is not a property of actors, but rather something which is inherent in the fabric of society, inherent in the relationships between actors. This kind of analysis has been developed in part because of the difficulties associated with discovering the power of given actors and the fact that some actors seem to get what they want despite having no obvious source of power or power base.

One argument is that different types of political situation lead to different types of outcomes. Here the nature of the relations between actors, which define the type of political situation, is correlated with different sorts of outcome. Regime theory is an example of such accounts of structural or systemic power. Stone argues that in different cities in the USA, different regimes exist. The type of regime in any given city shapes policy in that city, and furthermore the type of policy shapes the preferences of the actors in the regime. He believes the nature of the regime is far more important than the personal preferences of the actors within the regime.

An example from Atlanta shows that when the white administration was unable to expand the city boundaries to secure a white majority coalition, the business elite learned to cooperate with black political leaders in order to maintain their interests. Initially, the black leaders were suspicious of the business elite but soon learned that they were required in order to maintain the economic prosperity important to some of their own development plans for rundown parts of the city. On the assumption that white political leaders do not have a preference for working with black political leaders, and black political leaders' natural suspicion of the white business elite, Stone (1989: 160) claims that '*Regime analysis instructs us that policy innovation is not about individuals and their preferences*' (original emphasis). In fact, all we have here is a conflict of preferences. The white business community may have had a preference for working with white political leaders, but it had a stronger preference for working with an administration that could secure its development goals. Similarly, as Stone describes, the black leadership of Atlanta had an interest in securing certain benefits for its (largely black) supporters; it also found that these could more easily be secured through working with business to produce development. Of course, as Stone also describes, some of the development plans were opposed by the black administration's main supporters and so compromises had to be made all round. But that is part-and-parcel of the coalitional business of politics.

Stone (1980) created the concept of systemic power to try to explain how formal political equality and great social inequality through social stratification change political coalitions once they gain political power. The structures of society create incentives for governors to change their behaviour in order to achieve some of their aims. Furthermore, as their behaviour changes through interactions, so do their preferences, in much the way we saw is possible with repeated interaction of the Battle of the Sexes and other games. It is wrong to characterize this as 'systemic power'. It is not the system that has power, but the actors bargaining to achieve their aims as completely as possible. It is a mistake to think that because we are mapping the structure *of* power, that structures *have* power. Describing the distribution of power in society by the relations between people does not mean that the relations between those people are themselves powerful. The theory that structures have power may be dismissed by two complementary arguments: first, such ascriptions are redundant; second, they are misleading. The first may be called the *redundancy* argument, the second the *conceptual* argument (Dowding 1991: 8–9).

The redundancy argument. It is sometimes claimed that the physical structures of New York City's freeways embody racial and class bias. These structures therefore embody structural power (Winner 1980; Ward 1987b). Low-level bridges prevent buses from using some routes and so sections of the population without cars are effectively prevented from visiting parts of the city. Leaving aside the issue of why some people do not own cars, we have here a lack of outcome power of some people, not the power of the physical structures to prevent them. If I cannot go south because there is a wall in the way, then we may wish to say that the wall has the power to stop me going south. But we do not need to. All we need to say is that the wall stops me going south, which is a less long-winded way of saying the same thing (conceptually the sentences are equivalent). The use of the word 'power' here is redundant. Moreover, it is misleading.

The conceptual argument. The use of the word 'power' in this example is very different from the use of the word power when we talk of actors having power, and different in a way which makes the use of this abstract noun misleading (conceptually the usage is different). When we speak of the power of an individual, we are talking about a power that she may choose not to wield. If A has power over B to the extent that she can make him do x, then she can make B do x but she may choose not to bother. Structures do not have this ability to choose not to wield the power they may be thought to have. If the phrase 'structural' or 'systemic' power is to be used, then it needs to be carefully demarcated from ordinary uses of the term. Stone (1987a: 16) recognizes this when he writes 'Structural constraints are real, but they are mediated through the political arrangements that enable a prevailing coalition to govern a community . . . settings vary, and what community actors make of these settings varies as understandings change from one time and governing coalition to another'.

Even though individuals may choose not to wield the power that they have, their choice situation may make that non-wielding option unappealing. The fact that the structure of individual decision-making may make outcomes predictable with a high probability does not show that structures have power. It merely demonstrates that what individuals do is structurally suggested by their positions in society. An individual facing a single-play Prisoners' Dilemma will soon realize that not to cooperate with her fellow player is the rational course of action, for that choice strictly dominates the other. Choosing not to cooperate is strongly structurally suggested, though any player may choose, despite the realization that cooperating is dominated, to try to cooperate with her fellow player. In the Battle of the Sexes, the structural suggestion is less clear. Should I try to make my fellow player coordinate with my first preference, or should we coordinate with my fellow player's first preference? Structurally, the game still suggests action, but less strongly than in the Prisoners' Dilemma. A game in which all the outcomes were identical would not suggest any given course of action. If, for example, we do not know what our preferences are for all the possible outcomes (i.e. we do not know what the numbers are in the boxes in the matrix), then we may as well choose at random. At the end of the first part of Sartre's *Iron in the Soul*, Mathieu fired wildly at the approaching German army, trying to hold the parapet for 15 minutes. Each shot 'avenged some ancient scruple' (Sartre 1949: 225) as he imagined shooting at everything he hated, and everything he loved, and in doing so he felt cleansed, 'He was all-powerful, he was free'. Sartre's image here is of no constraint on Mathieu's actions, he did just as he wanted, or rather he acted almost without reason. Total freedom in Sartre's sense is random choice; having a reason for doing something is a recognition of the incentives to behave one way or another. True freedom for Sartre, then, is transcending even the constraints of reasons for action. Turning this on its head, one might think that acting for one's own reasons is what is meant by 'freedom', but reasons do not come to us unencumbered by the effects of the world around us. Our reasons develop from where we find ourselves situated. Structural suggestion is therefore not necessarily a constraint upon freedom; it can also enable free choice, for without it we may not be able to develop reasons for, or have any interests to motivate, action.

The New York freeway example is not, in any case, a very good example of structural power. Robert Moses helped set up the Triborough Bridge Authority to produce a controlled number of toll roads and bridges in a high-volume traffic area. This created a set of captive consumers buying a private good without taking into account the negative externalities of pollution, environmental damage, urban sprawl and over half a million people displaced by highways. By creating a quasi-private authority, the Moses empire was protected from close public scrutiny. How far Moses was aware of all the externalities of the system he helped build is moot; he may even have deliberately created the inequalities his roads aggravated (Caro 1974). This would enable us to say that it was Moses' power which caused the inequality of movement. Certainly, Moses has often been held up as a good example of a powerful elite actor (Molotch 1976; Stone 1987b). Even if the inequalities were an unintended consequence or a by-product of Moses' actions, the point, if this is to be an example of structural power, is that the structure itself does not have power. It is simply that the structures reduce the power of some groups to take certain actions. A reduction in one person's power does not entail an increase in the power of someone or something else. To think so is to commit the blame fallacy. We can see this by considering the collective action problem.

The collective action problem

The overall interests of an individual may not be secured through self-interested actions. We saw this in some of the games in Chapter 1. Collective action problems emerge especially for large groups of individuals who find it difficult to coordinate their actions to secure their group interest. This problem was brought to the attention of political scientists by Mancur Olson, who wrote:

> unless the number of individuals in a group is quite small, or unless there is coercion or some other special device to make individuals act in their common interest, *rational, self-interested individuals will not act to achieve their common or group interests*.
>
> (Olson 1971: 2)

The collective action problem is now well known in political science, yet it is still misunderstood. Many writers who have tried to challenge the Olsonian wisdom of there being genuine problems involved in the mobilization of large numbers of people to secure their collective self-interest have failed to understand that collective action is a problem, not an impossibility. Many of those who have tried to 'answer Olson' have demonstrated the truth of his claim by accepting that there is a problem worth resolving in the first place. There are many obstacles in the way of large numbers of people acting to secure their collective self-interest. Understanding the different problems which emerge for people in securing their interests is important in understanding power, because these problems affect the power of groups to act in ways consistent with their interests, even if there is no-one else trying to stop them. Groups have differential abilities to mobilize, based upon properties of the group, not upon the opposition of other groups. Understanding the power structure entails understanding the nature of these different features of groups to see why they are not all equally able to pursue their own interests.

The collective action problem encompasses 'demand-side problems' and 'supply-side solutions'. The first generates the sorts of problems of collective action for which public choice and game theory are best known. The major aspects of the demand-side problem are the nature of the production function, the nature of the interest held in common and the characteristics of the group. Sometimes these three aspects of the demand side entail hardly any problem of collective action at all. Sometimes, however, they denote a problem of such force that it is difficult to see a solution providing for stable long-term collective action. This should make clear that there is no such thing as *the* collective action problem, though many people (including at times myself) have written as though there was only one problem. There are collective action problems, but as the difficulties are plural, so are the solutions.

The final part of this chapter provides a brief overview of the supply-side solutions, showing how some groups, largely because of the nature of the group itself, have differing abilities to overcome their particular collective action problems. These solutions are dependent upon the characteristics of the particular collective action problem they address and do not all apply to all mobilization situations. They show how groups are able to gain more power in the social bargaining game.

Demand-side problems

Each of the demand-side problems will be listed and discussed briefly. It will be seen that they are interlinked and interrelated.

1 *The 'free-rider' problem.* The problems of collective action are often seen simply as the 'free-rider' problem. However, the free-rider problem is narrower than the totality of collective action problems and I will provide a very narrow conception here. It exists wherever there is non-excludability. The condition of non-excludability is often given as a defining feature of a 'collective good' but is actually entailed by other characteristics (Dowding and Dunleavy, in press). A collective good was identified by Samuelson (1954, 1955) as one which leads in particular to problems of market supply. Collective goods are defined by a bundle of characteristics, including 'jointness of supply' or 'non-rivalness' (i.e. if they are supplied to one person in a group, they are supplied to everyone) and non-excludability (i.e. it is uneconomic to stop someone from enjoying the good).[1] These characteristics mean that it is harder to make profits by

supplying collective goods than it is by supplying private goods, so capitalists tend to fight shy of providing them. If they see a profitable way of doing this, however, they may well do so. Samuelson argued that because of the supply problems of collective goods, government often needs to step in. The condition of jointness of supply or non-rivalness may lead to a degree of non-exclusion where excluding individuals from enjoying the benefits (or disutilities) of a good is economically infeasible (i.e. it is not profitable to do so). The degree of jointness, and therefore non-excludability, is crucially dependent upon current technology and other economic conditions. Some goods may have been non-excludable in the past, but are excludable today. It may not be worthwhile for firms to supply goods under certain economic conditions, but other conditions may make it profitable. The technological and economic circumstances conditioning the characteristics of economic goods are not always well understood and many writers have attempted to produce universal definitions good for all times and all places. It should also be recognized that non-excludability often exists simply by law, where states have determined that certain goods and services are universal by right, even though exclusion is both naturally and economically feasible. Non-excludability entails the 'free-rider' problem, since a rational self-interested utility maximizer will see no benefit in contributing towards a collective good that she will receive anyway. If I have a right to police protection, then I will see no benefit in voluntarily paying for police services. Coercive taxation is the usual state response. Note that such calculations rely crucially on the assumption that I will receive the good whether or not I pay for it. A supply-side response, as we shall see, is to attempt to convince would-be free-riders that if they do not contribute they will not receive the good, not through exclusion, but because the good will not be provided at all. In this sense, jointness of supply cuts both ways. It provides both a reason, via non-excludability, for not paying and a reason to encourage collective action where the good of sufficient quality is not forthcoming.

2 *Recognition of interests.* It may appear obvious that individuals will not act to secure their own interests if they are not aware they have them. A great deal of effort is expended on the supply

side to convince individuals that their interests are best served by one course of action rather than another. It should also be acknowledged that even where there is no free-rider problem and individuals are in a positive-sum coordination game, as in Figures 1.1(b) and 1.2, they will not cooperate unless they are aware that it is a positive-sum coordination game. Recognition of interests is thus vital. What is less well recognized, at least by formal theorists, is that the very structure of decision situations may make interest recognition harder to achieve. This is often exploited by those with contrary interests (Dowding 1991).

3 *The relative costs* of taking part in collective action are important. Olson's (1971) algebraic argument is that individuals will not contribute towards a collective good if the extra benefits they enjoy through receiving that good are worth less than the costs of contributing. This argument depends crucially upon the nature of the production function. If the good is perfectly jointly supplied, then Olson's algebra is irrelevant (Marwell and Oliver 1993) and depends upon actors relating the extra increment of the good supplied to the contribution they make towards its provision. The richer the group, the lower the relative costs of the good to them. It is also worth noting that typically consumers assign parts of their expenditure to different types of good; some for needs such as food and clothing, some for transport, some for luxury items and so on. They may be thought also to assign some part for gifts, some for charitable donations and some for group aims. We should expect the assignations to be in part dependent upon the needs items being provided first. Thus we should expect large asymmetries in amounts set aside for group aims across social classes.

4 *Group size*. The larger the group, the harder it is to coordinate group activities. This insight is still important, though its impact has perhaps been exaggerated as other factors about groups may override this component. Group size is important in two senses: first, the degree of perceptibility of individual contributions (Olson 1971; Barry 1978) increases the free-rider problem and may be considered a problem of coordination; secondly, the actual importance of any given contribution must be taken into account (Olson 1971; Taylor 1987). The larger the group, the less important an individual contribution may appear to group success. The degree of perceptibility is more dependent upon interactiveness (see (6) below) than size as such.

5 *Group homogeneity.* The more homogeneous the group, the easier it is to discover any shared preferences, the fewer the cross-cutting cleavages, and thus the sources of conflict within the group. Homogeneity in another sense may work in another direction. If the group is heterogeneous in wealth terms, then it may be easier to secure collective action to the degree that very rich members may make the good virtually privileged in Olson's terms (see Marwell and Oliver 1993, for discussion of this type of homogeneity).

6 *Group interactiveness.* The degree of interaction between group members is more important than group size *per se* (Truman 1951; Hardin 1982; Marwell and Oliver 1993). Olson has a very unrealistic picture of group interaction, seemingly imagining that in order for a group of a certain size (g) to begin to mobilize, a certain subgroup of size k must form, and that the relationship between k and g is important. However, face-to-face interaction among a small group of people may lead to subgroup mobilization no matter how large the wider group. Many of the size problems first elucidated by Olson can be and are overcome by interaction within smaller subgroups (Hardin 1982).

7 *Opposition.* The opposition to a particular group forming is also important in the very beginning of mobilization. The fact of a rival group organizing itself successfully can act as a spur to collective action (Moe 1980; Hirschman 1983; Walker 1983). But opposing groups can also act to stultify the mobilization in the early stages (Dowding 1991). They can exploit cross-cutting cleavages within the group to try to break up the coalition of interests (Riker 1982), they can try to preference-shape the group away from the common interest coagulation (Dunleavy 1991), they can make the costs of mobilizing higher by numerous strategies depending upon the relationship between the rival forces.

8 *The number of non-rival demands.* Individuals have a large number of interests and causes they support. In the case of charities, there may be a wide range of causes that I am prepared to support. However, my utility function can be imagined to set aside only certain amounts for such donations. Greenpeace, Oxfam, Save the Children, Cancer Research Fund and so on are all in competition in their demands upon the 'group donation' end of my utility function. Obviously they are rivals for my money, but can be described as non-rival in my affections. I am

prepared to support them all and do not see their ends as being competitive against one another. The number of such non-rival demands will affect the degree of success of any organization. This claim could have policy implications for organizations with membership subscriptions. More organizations are moving towards encouraging members to pay by direct debit or standing order. Given that such subscriptions involve no costs in paying over and beyond the amount donated itself, but are costly in time and trouble to cancel (especially direct debits), they help to maintain membership. However, organizations also like to have their subscriptions start on the first day of the year, with subscriptions falling due in December. This entails greater competition for subscriptions to non-rival organizations and could lead to a loss of membership over all such organizations, and hence a collective action problem for charitable organizations.

9 *Increasing or decreasing well-being.* There is little theoretical or empirical agreement on the effects of increasing or decreasing well-being. To some extent, an increase in wealth makes collective action more likely, for it decreases the relative costs. A burgeoning middle class, for example, may make more demands upon the state for certain types of collective good or may be more ready to defend its interests. It also appears that decreasing well-being may spark revolutionary collective action as peasants revolt against falling standards of living. Perhaps as conditions worsen, the costs of revolution (dying) do not seem so bad when death through starvation or state oppression seems quite probable without revolutionary action.

10 *Continual or 'one-off'.* A very different production function is created by the nature of the collective good. 'One-off' goods are typified by the step function illustrated in Figure 2.2, though the step may not be as discontinuous as appears here. Continuous goods provide a different type of collective action or coordination problem and it may be hypothesized that the nature of the membership of an organization providing continual action may be very different from that of an organization providing a step good (Kimber 1993). For some organizations such as charities, membership turnover might be expected to be relatively high, whereas others more concerned with self-interest of members, such as trades unions, should be more stable.

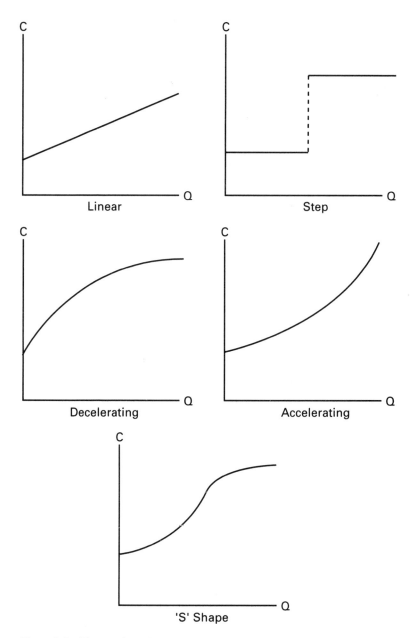

Figure 2.2   Types of goods.

11 *Coordination*. The coordinating of activities is a key factor. The degree to which coordination is required is in part dependent upon many of the above factors. A small group where there are few cross-cutting cleavages and costs are small may only require coordination of activities. Larger groups, with a greater hetero-geneity and relatively high costs, may require coordination of a much higher order where the costs to the coordinator will be correspondingly higher. This is a problem on the demand side which provokes various supply-side answers, to be considered below.

We can see, therefore, that the characteristics of the group affect its ability to mobilize its members to secure common aims. Different groups in society have different powers simply by virtue of group characteristics. Some of these characteristics are properties of the individuals that comprise the group, but others are properties of the group itself, rather than its individual members. An individual's outcome power is thus also affected by the character-istics of the group of which she is a member as well as her own abilities if she is only able to attain some of her desires through collective action. Solutions to these collective action problems may be found.

Supply-side solutions

There are a number of aspects of the supply side which aid collective action. We will begin by considering some of the actions of the state which facilitate mobilization. These are often ignored in formal discussion of collective action, which outside the context of revolutions tends to take the liberal state for granted.

1 *The state*. The state enables collective action by the rights it gives for group mobilization. The rights to free speech, freedom of expression, to form organizations and to represent common interests, all decrease the costs of mobilization (or, conversely, their absence increases the costs: formally this makes no differ-ence). The state may intervene more directly. It may help to finance organizations either directly, such as the state funding of political parties in Germany, or through tax incentives, which exist (in different forms) for charities in, for example, Britain and the USA. The state also lowers or increases the costs of

mobilization on the supply side by the degree of openness it displays towards lobbying and bargaining efforts. If the state is perceived to be relatively open to persuasion and lobbying, then it is more worthwhile forming organizations to lobby. If it seems relatively closed or uninterested in certain types of political demand, then organizations may find mobilization harder. Of course, in liberal societies, many organizations begin by lobbying public opinion before turning attention to government, which becomes less indifferent to issues as the general public begins to demonstrate some concern. The degree of freedom and the rights individuals enjoy are an important source of their power.

2 *Political entrepreneurs and political movers.* In order to overcome coordination difficulties, some actor or set of actors may need to step in. A political entrepreneur (Frohlich and Oppenheimer 1970; Frohlich *et al.* 1971) is a person who can see a potential profit in coordinating collective action. This may be related to their other activities. Chong (1991) argues that black church leaders found themselves drawn into the civil rights movement in the 1960s in order to secure the continued support of their parishioners. Church leaders who were vocal in organizing for civil rights drew greater congregations than those who were silent. The competition for congregations thus led church leaders into becoming civil rights leaders too. But that is not to say that they were drawn in against their will, nor that they did not 'really' support civil rights. The idea of the political mover is that he or she is someone less interested in personal profit from the activities of an organization than the political entrepreneur, but rather sees personal gain simply in terms of the provision of the collective good. To some extent, the appearance of an entrepreneur or a political mover may be entirely contingent and not subject to theoretical generalizing.[2] However, we can hypothesize that certain types of common interest may generate greater profitable opportunities than others. Schneider *et al.* (1995) and Clark and Goetz (1994) have demonstrated that certain sets of conditions are correlated with the emergence of local political entrepreneurs in urban politics. Similarly, group heterogeneity may increase the chances of a political mover emerging to the extent that some group members have a greater interest in seeking successful coordination than others. It should also be noted that while the self-interest axiom in rational choice has

proved somewhat disturbingly successful in predictive modelling, it is of course false. There are many altruistic people around, and most of us, even if we are self-interested most of the time, regularly indulge in altruistic acts. If we imagine a certain probability of altruistic activity across a group, we might expect, despite its higher costs, that a political coordinator is more likely to emerge than spontaneous contributions towards some common end. Given that overcoming the coordination problem may significantly increase the chances of success, an individual prepared to be altruistic just once may calculate that the role of political mover is rational in a given case.

3 *Selective incentives* are Olson's solution to the collective action problem. It has been shown (Frohlich *et al.* 1971; Marsh 1976; Olson 1982) that selective incentives cannot fulfil, *on their own*, the central role assigned to them by Olson. Nevertheless, they are an important aspect of the solution to the free-rider problem. Many organizations provide selective incentives on top of the collective good, but selective incentives cannot be the main motivation of members of an organization primarily devoted to lobbying.

4 *Joint action*. One important source of mobilization occurs through joint action where one group supports another. An organization may see benefits in creating another organization with convergent interests. Sears Roebuck, a major supplier of agricultural equipment, has long provided material support to various farmers' organizations in the USA.

5 *Mock organizations*. Joint action taken to its furthest extreme leads to mock organizations created by one group to further the aims of another. For example, FOREST is largely a front organization for cigarette and tobacco companies, while major food manufacturers in Britain have set up several 'consumer groups' concerned with quality of produce. Greater regulation of the quality of food is to the advantage of the larger food manufacturers. Consumer rights may here be promoted as a by-product of the interests of large food manufacturers, though some would argue that such regulatory capture is, overall, against consumer interests.

6 *Advertising causes*. One of the major activities of group organiz-ations is to advertise the cause and attempt to persuade people of their interests and preferences with regard to the activities of the

organization. This is the major way of overcoming the preference realization problem. Organizations tend to run through a cycle of first advertising their cause to attract membership and persuade public opinion, then turning attention to more direct 'insider' lobbying activities if they are able to get their demands on to the government's policy agenda.

The incentives for activists on the supply side vary. Some may be entrepreneurial, setting up organizations largely for personal gain, much as entrepreneurs engage in economic activity in the private sector. Some may be less entrepreneurial and may set up an organization for group ends, still self-interested, in the sense that the 'political mover' is a member of the group, but not purely for personal profit. Such political movers may prefer that some other actor performed the coordination role but take it on when they see that the role is not going to be performed and therefore the good not produced (Oliver 1984). The coordinator may be motivated by truly altruistic reasons. Finally, of course, most people who work in organizations do so because it is their job. They are paid employees.

Collective action and political power

Groups do not have to face explicit opposition in order to be powerless – they first have to overcome their peculiar collective action problems. Groups face different sorts of collective action problems depending not only on the characteristics of the individuals in the group, but also on the nature of their collective interest and the characteristics of the group itself. The nature of these problems may be dependent upon the actions of other individuals and groups in the past, but need not have developed through strategic deliberate manipulation of others. Once mobilized, groups may face explicit opposition and some groups will mobilize in response to the mobilization of others. The collective action problem is at the heart of all considerations of the power structure. It generates the divergence of power between different groups according to the differing resources and conditions of groups of people.

How structures change people

One of the most forceful aspects of structural accounts of power is where they suggest that power lies outside actors, controlling seemingly powerful people as much as they control others. In one of his more lucid passages, Foucault (1980: 156), discussing Bentham's Panopticon (a plan for an efficient prison), says:

> One doesn't have here a power which is wholly in the hands of one person who can exercise it alone and totally over the others. It's a machine in which everyone is caught, those who exercise power just as much as those over whom it is exercised.

We can understand how people, both the powerless and the powerful, get caught up in 'the system' of which they are a part. Some collective action problems may be so great that we feel completely powerless to do anything. The sense of powerlessness that structures can engender can be seen in Steinbeck's *The Grapes of Wrath*, where the tenant threatens to shoot Joe Davis's boy driving the tractor that will pull down his house. But he realizes they'll just hang him for it and someone else will drive the tractor. Killing the man who gave Davis's boy the orders will not help, for he is just carrying out the orders of the bank, and the bank gets its orders from the East, and they aren't ordering anyone to pull down the house, just to ensure that the bank does not go under with the weight of debt it is carrying.

This is the force of structures. It is not that people are not acting. It is not that they cannot act any other way. It is not that there is no-one with power: everyone has some power, and some more than others, but no one person is required for the end to occur. No one person is *the* cause, and thus personally responsible for the bad or good outcomes. Each person finds themselves in situations that structurally suggest one course of action or another, but they may know that if only they and others could act in concert some other outcome might accrue. Each person's action affects others; indeed, one person's action is (a part of) another's structure.

But the structure not only affects the way that people act, it also affects the way they *are*. Structures go right down deep into the heart and mind of each person. We saw how difficult it is to decide what are the 'real' preferences of the man and the woman in the repeated Battle of the Sexes game, as they each respond to the other's behaviour and their own attitudes towards each other change. But as people feel compelled to do that which they feel is wrong, this may hurt them. Not everyone is the same, and not all react the same to the compulsion of structure, but each is changed. Steinbeck (1939: 30) describes this better than I can:

Some of the owner men were kind because they hated what they had to do, and some of them were angry because they hated to be cruel, and some of them were cold because they had long ago found that one could not be an owner unless one were cold. And all of them hated the mathematics that drove them, and some were afraid, and some worshipped the mathematics because it provided a refuge from thought and from feeling.

Modern management textbooks and courses for senior and middle managers now teach that you should not become friends with those below you, because one day you may have to discipline or fire them. They also teach how to behave machine-like when getting rid of staff: give them 15 minutes to clear their desks, have them escorted from the building by security staff, behave coldly. The idea is to ensure that when you are firing someone you do not let yourself become upset; behaving machine-like is a defence mechanism for your own psyche. How else could humans systematically lead others to gas-chambers? These are stark examples of how situations change people, how structures lead us to willingly or unwillingly change our personalities and characters in order to deal with the world around us. But these stark examples are just illustrative of the pressures that are upon us all the time. How can one ever know what is in our 'real' interests? My recommended method for trying to understand what real interests are only suggests that we can know at times that it is not in our real interests to be in the situations in which we find ourselves. But we can never know that where we are situated is the 'best' position in which to find 'ourselves' because 'ourselves' is partly constituted by the position we are in. However, that does not mean that we cannot judge our position in relation to the situation of others, or judge our position in relation to what it might be. It is these latter calculations that matter, for it is these calculations that lead us to try to make the world a better place for ourselves. We need to further examine the structures productive of power, and discover that they are not only productive of power, but also of luck.

Notes

1 Collective goods are defined differently by different people, but these two characteristics will suffice here. See Sandler (1992) or Dowding and Dunleavy (in press) for more extensive discussions of collective goods.
2 See Dowding (1991: 89–103) for discussion of the importance of political movers in the case studies of Crenson (1971) and Gaventa (1980).

3
Luck and Power

In Chapter 1, we saw how the relationship between two actors can be represented in a game form. This relationship suggests the possibilities of action to the players, and indicates what the best course of action is for each. I called this 'structural suggestion', since, together with the players' preference orderings, it was the nature of the game, defined in terms of the relationships between the players, which suggests the best course of action to each player. Sometimes this course of action is strongly suggested, as with the concept of dominance in the single-play Prisoners' Dilemma. Sometimes, as in the repeated Battle of the Sexes, the suggestion may be quite weak. When the course of action is strongly suggested, then the actors have little room for manoeuvre. It is in these conditions that writers sometimes talk about structural determination, when life makes an offer we can't refuse, and it is these conditions that lead some writers to want to describe structures as having power, since if everyone's best course of action is manifested by the way the world is, then each person seems to have no choice in the matter and therefore no power. In Chapter 2, I argued that to write of structural power is a mistake, first because the word 'power' does not do any work (the redundancy argument) and, secondly, since even when the conditions are such that we seem to have no choice, those conditions cannot decide to not enforce themselves (the conceptual argument). Furthermore, even when we 'have no choice', that phrase is being used metaphorically. The 'no choice' we have means that the best course of action seems obvious, but in reality we still have to *choose* that obvious course of action. The proof of this is that we can still choose not to follow the obvious course of action. Deciding not to cooperate with your fellow prisoner in a Prisoners' Dilemma may be the dominant strategy, but each prisoner can still say 'to hell with that' and honourably, stupidly or even ignorantly (not realizing it is the dominant strategy) refuse to help the police. If both do it, then both are better off than both choosing the dominant strategy. Structural suggestion may be strong, but it is never determinate.

In this chapter, we will consider accounts of power which maintain that the structure of society determines the power of everyone and thus the way society runs. These arguments imply that in capitalist society capitalists will always win. The power structure is controlled by an elite consisting of businesspeople, leading politicians and bureaucrats who intermingle through both familial and class backgrounds, but largely because of their functional roles. We shall see that while structural determinism is too strong a phrase, there is a great deal of structural suggestion. This does not simply lead to elites having greater powers than everyone else. Their power is based upon their resources, and their resource-base may be defined in structural terms. However, elites tend to get what they want as much through luck as through actually wielding power, though they may keep their power in reserve for when it is needed.

In Chapter 1, we defined some people as being lucky in their games, since the situation they find themselves in places them at an advantage compared with other players. This chapter extends the account of luck. The players in the different games all faced different possibilities of attaining their favoured payoffs. Some had the opportunities to work together to secure positive payoffs for each, some were in straightforward conflict situations (constant-sum games) where one player's loss was another's gain, while others had the possibility of cooperation open to them despite conflict lurking below the surface. I suggested that the players who were facing pure coordination games were lucky, while those in the conflict situations were unlucky, especially those players like Player 1 in Figure 1.1(a) whose best response will only get him his third-most preferred payoff. The insight behind the false conception of structural power is that our power is constrained by the opportunities which lie open to us. I want to capture this by developing the concept of luck.

Pivotality

In a famous article, Brian Barry (1991) asked if it was better to be powerful or lucky. The short answer is both. But the long answer suggests that if one gets what one wants without trying, then why should one want power? Furthermore, the amount of power that one actually has is partly built on luck. In order to develop this insight, we need to look at the attempts to measure power through a power index.

There are many different power indices. They do not all measure power equally (in fact I do not think they measure power at all, but 'voting resources'; see below). Here I wish to consider only the Shapley–Shubik index on which Brian Barry builds his account of luck (Shapley and Shubik 1969; Shapley 1967, 1981). The Shapley–Shubik power index attempts to measure the outcome power of individual members on a committee. They try to capture this causal notion by asking the question, 'When is the individual voter decisive in securing her preferred outcome?'. They imagine a group of actors all willing to vote for some measure. Each person votes one after the other until a bare majority is reached, the voting ceases and the measure is declared passed. The last person to vote for the measure is credited with being decisive, her vote having secured the bare majority. This person is called the *pivotal voter* or *pivot*. It is important to note that this scheme is not meant to represent a real voting system, it is simply a device to try to capture the causal notion underlying the outcome power of voters. The full outcome power of each voter is then given by how often each is, or could be, the pivotal voter. The pivot can then be defined:

$$P_i = m(i)/n!$$

Where P is the power of the voter i in a set of voters $\{1, 2, \ldots, n\}$ and $m(i)$ is the number of times that i is *pivotal* in securing that outcome ($n!$ means n factorial and if $n = 4$ then $4! = 4 \times 3 \times 2 \times 1 = 24$). Being pivotal is defined as follows. When the voting rules define q votes as a winning number,

$$(n+1) \le q \le n \text{ or } n/2 + 1 \le q \le n$$

The pivotal position is the qth position in any ordered sequence of votes, there being $n!$ ordered sequences. Thus:

$$\sum_{i=1}^{n} P_i = 1$$

Under this definition, a voter's power is determined by the number of times she is pivotal in relation to the number of possible ordered sequences. In other words, the power of any given voter is the probability that that individual is the final member of a minimum winning coalition. The power of all members of a committee always sums to 1.

For a committee of three people, *a, b, c*, the potential ordering of votes is:

abc
acb
bac
bca
cab
cba

In each case, the middle voter is pivotal. As *a, b* and *c* are each the middle voter twice, there are six orderings and thus $i/n! = 2/6 = 1/3$. Thus each voter in a committee of three has Shapley–Shubik power to the amount of 1/3. This may seem a rather long-winded way of discovering a trivial result. However, in a system of one voter one vote, this is the result we should find, so at least we can feel that the method is getting the correct answer. The method provides less trivial results when we consider weighted voting, where the number of votes each voter gets is not equal. Imagine that *a, b* and *c* are three parties in a legislature of 100 members. Party *a* has 49 members, party *b* 48 members and party *c* 3 members. The set of winning sequences is as above, and each party has an equal power, for despite the fact that both parties *a* and *b* have far more votes than party *c*, they still require *c* in order to form a majority. Here party *c*, in Shapley–Shubik terms, is as powerful as either *a* or *b*. Now the result seems less trivial, for it shows that small parties in legislatures often have power well beyond their apparent voting strength.

However, this example, while demonstrating the importance of the pivot, and of how one's Shapley–Shubik power may not be immediately apparent in a simple comparison of voting resources, may also make us suspicious of the index as a measure of *power*.

While we can see that party c is required in order for either a or b to win majority votes, we would not expect that in a real parliament party c would have the same power as either a or b. The intuition is correct. The number of times a voter is a pivot in any possible sequence of votes tells us how often that voter could wield power if it is known he is a pivot in the Shapley–Shubik sense. But that is not the same as that voter's power. We can see this using an example of someone who, as luck would have it, is always a pivot.

The US Supreme Court has nine Justices. Studies of the Court have shown that Justices tend to vote on ideological issues as might be predicted from their reputation as liberals or conservatives (Segal and Cover 1989). Imagine there are four conservatives and four liberals and each bloc votes together on ideological issues. There is one Justice who sometimes votes with the conservatives and sometimes with the liberals. We call him the Maverick Justice (MJ). On each case before the Court, there are only two possible verdicts: either in favour of the plaintiff or in favour of the defendant. It might be thought that MJ has more power than other Justices on all ideological votes, since he gets what he wants 100 per cent of the time, whereas the others only get what they want, say, 50 per cent of the time (Barry 1988: 345). Can we really make this claim? MJ only appears to have more power than the other Justices because he gets what he wants twice as often as everyone else. But is getting what you want the same as power? If MJ happened to vote with the conservatives all the time, then MJ would still get what he wanted 100 per cent of the time. Does he have the same power as he had before, even though he is now just one member of a five-member conservative bloc? Now he seems to have no more power than the four conservatives. Would we then say that these five had equal power and the four liberals no power? Not by the Shapley–Shubik power index. MJ only appears to have more power by the fact that in the example he is the pivotal voter as defined by the preference structure – we said he was MJ. He can only get what he wants on each vote if there are four other Justices who agree with him. There may be votes off the conservative–liberal ideological dimension where he loses 8 to 1. He only appears more powerful because the preferences of the other two blocs are taken as given but his is not. When MJ votes with one of the two blocs, then any of the four Justices in that bloc has an equal claim to be pivotal. MJ may be able to claim to be pivotal 100 per cent of the time, the other eight Justices only 50 per cent of the time; but that does not give MJ more power, for the other Justices *could* scupper his plans each time. The fact that in the example they do not shows nothing, for what matters in questions of power is what they *can* do, not what they do do. We saw this in Chapter 1 when we realized that I may have the outcome power to throw a stone 50 metres even if I never actually do throw it. We might say that MJ is lucky that he gets what he wants all the time, but luck is not the same as power.

We might try to dispute this account of power on the grounds that the actual preferences of the Justices are relevant to their actual power in votes. Peter Morriss (1987) argues that in social science we are interested in the power of people given the environment they inhabit, not the power that people might have in some counter-actual sense:

> The rich are able to feed off caviar and champagne; the poor have to restrict themselves to beer and pickles, and are unable to eat more expensive food. This is not due to any lack of masticatory ability on their part, but because of the social and economic environment they inhabit. They are unable to eat caviar, whilst having the ability to do so.
>
> (Morriss 1987: 81)

Here Morriss is trading on a difference between what he calls 'ability' – the quality in an agent which makes action possible – and 'ableness', derived from the sense of being able or being in such a position that the thing is possible for one. Ability in this example is simply masticatory ability. The poor have the ability to eat caviar if they steal it, or stage a revolution after which it is equally rationed. If they cannot steal it because it is too closely guarded, and do not revolt for they have worked out that the costs of revolting are greater than the rewards of having a portion of fish roe each week, then they may remain unable to eat caviar. But here their inability to eat caviar is based on their abilities. Their resources do not allow them to buy caviar, to steal it, or to be bothered to stage a revolution. These are abilities every bit as much as their masticatory ones.

The Maverick Justice may seem like the rich getting what he wants, and the other eight Justices the poor, waiting on the actions of the rich to see if they get what they want. However, this is to confuse outcomes with resources. The Maverick Justice only has one vote just like the others. His power base is the same as theirs: he is simply lucky that his preferences and everyone else's line up as they do. If this were not so, then four of the other Justices could gain power by saying that they would always ensure their preferences lined up with the Maverick Justice, so they too always got what they wanted. But this is ridiculous. Power cannot be getting what you vote for if that does not correspond to what you want. Having power is getting what you want, not wanting what you can get. Those like Morriss (1987: 169) who want to produce a power index which measures the predicted pattern of votes given the pattern of preferences of a committee are confusing the structural base of the power of voters, demonstrated in a Shapley–Shubik index, with the individual desire to have one outcome rather than another. Power indices can measure power based upon voting resources; they should not be made to measure luck or power based on other resources.

Happening to be pivotal or being lucky that one is pivotal brings power, but these circumstances are not themselves a source of power; rather it is the *realization* that one is pivotal which brings power. In other words, being pivotal is itself a *resource* which may be used by the holder to a greater or lesser extent. If the Maverick Justice votes entirely on his preferences, then he has no greater claim to be pivotal than the others, for he is behaving just as they are. Any one of the five winners on each vote can claim to be pivotal (that is, none is), for they are mathematically indistinguishable except by definition. The greater power of pivotal voters – for example, small parties in hung parliaments – comes about not because they happen to vote one way or another, but because their actions change with the realization that they are pivotal. Pivotal voters behave differently from non-pivotal ones. They can use the fact of their crucial position in order to achieve a greater number of outcomes than they otherwise could. (Not necessarily a greater number than non-pivotal voters – large parties still write most of the legislation in hung parliaments – but more than the pivotal voter could have got if she were non-pivotal with the same amount of luck.)

Pivotal power leads smaller parties to bargain with larger parties to achieve some of their desired outcomes. The larger party may agree to introduce some legislation that the smaller party desires in return for general support to keep it in power. A small party may bargain for a few cabinet seats and control over some policy areas in return for supporting the larger party in power. This bargaining power derives from the pivotal position of the smaller party. To return to a committee of nine structured as the Supreme Court with two power blocs of four and a maverick pivotal voter who can bargain with each bloc to get some outcomes she wants, the maverick committee member will only choose to support one bloc or another on each vote according to (a) her preferences with regard to the issue in question, and (b) whether she can persuade either bloc to agree to vote for other policies which she wants in return for her support on this issue. The measure of her power is how much she can get of what she wants through her ability to bargain with the two blocs. If she can get everything she wants simply by voting with either of the blocs on each issue, then she is just exceptionally lucky; but her *power* is her capacity to get new issues on to the agenda and to push through those policies she supports. She may vote with one bloc on one issue to which she is relatively indifferent or even opposed, as long as the strength of her dislike of those policies is less than the strength of her desire for the issues she is able to get on to the agenda. Blocs can also act strategically, so they can act as pivots.

Pivotality in this sense is thus a *resource* which brings power beyond one's voting strength. It is not what is meant by 'pivotality' in the Shapley–Shubik sense which is simply a formal device for measuring one's voting resources. But pivotality in this broader sense is based upon one's pivotality in the Shapley–Shubik sense together with the actual preferences of all the voters. How one makes use of this resource depends upon one's other resources or how good the maverick voter is at using her pivotal position. There are many important tactics one might use. One key tactic would be to hide one's true preferences from the other committee members. One might pretend to be very reluctant to agree to vote funds for a new dining room when in fact that is just what one wants, because one wants the others to agree to fund an extension to the car park. By pretending one is reluctant, one can force others to buy one's vote. Understanding the strategic issues involved and having the ability to carry them off is an important resource in bargaining games.

The Shapley–Shubik index approach to power is good at measuring the voting resources of individual voters, or blocs of voters who vote together. Its problem as an approach to power *per se* is that it denotes pivotality simply by definition. The flaw of the index approach to power is that it concentrates too much upon outcomes and not enough upon power as such (Barry 1991). Often one gets what one wants through luck.

Distinguishing luck and power

If the conservative bloc on the Supreme Court has a clear majority of, say, six to three, then as a group the conservatives are clearly powerful. On all ideological issues they can get what they want. However, each conservative Justice, as an individual, has exactly the same power as every other, and as each of the liberal Justices – that is, one vote each. Or, rather more carefully, we can say that each Justice has the same formal voting resource as every other: one vote each.

Barry will agree with the careful sentence, but not with the former one, for he believes that political power is getting what you want despite resistance (Barry 1991: 272; cf Weber 1978: 53). Powerful groups and people may not be able to carry out their precise will in any given situation, but they may be able to move the decision in the general direction of their will. Just getting what you want is not enough to demonstrate power, for one may simply be lucky. Barry defines luck as the probability of getting what you want without trying. Success is how often one gets what one wants if one tries. The difference between success and luck is an individual's decisiveness. So success = luck + decisiveness. Thus the notion that Shapley–Shubik were trying to develop with the number of sequences in which some voter is pivotal divided by the number of possible sequences is, in Barry's terms, a measure of their decisiveness. And, like the Shapley–Shubik power index, for any given individual each of these measures will take a value between 0 and 1, but the scores of all members do not have to sum to 1.

Barry believes that power is not like luck, success or decisiveness, in that it is a capability not a probability. Luck, success and decisiveness are not usually thought of as probabilities either. One's success is ordinarily thought to be getting what one wants, not the probability of getting what one wants. Similarly, luck is not normally considered to be the probability of getting what you want without trying, rather it is getting what you want when the probability of getting it is low. Decisiveness is defined by Barry as the increase in the probability of getting what you want if you try, whereas in this context it would ordinarily be thought to be a property of the person who tips the balance. Defining terms differently from how they are ordinarily defined is no problem. They can be thought of as technical definitions and what matters to a technical definition is whether, conceptually, it makes sense. But why can we not handle power in this way? While appreciating that power is a capability, we may still define it rather clumsily as 'the probability of getting what you want if you act in all possible worlds which are the same as the actual one with the exception of the preferences of all other actors'. This definition retains the capability aspect of power while building in a probabilistic analysis of an actor's success as a result of his capacities. It retains the capability aspect because it recognizes outcomes which you want as being a result of your actions rather than of luck. It does not include luck in the actual world, for the definition covers success in all possible worlds, thus including those worlds in which he is not lucky enough to get the outcomes he wants. Thus this definition recognizes that, while I may be lucky in this world and get what I want without having to act, I am still powerful because, if not lucky, I would have achieved my aims through my actions. It is, of course, possible to be powerful as well as lucky.

The decisiveness and luck of an actor vary according to the preferences of other actors, but an actor's power remains the same. It is a disposition, analysable counteractually by taking into account possible preference changes. This formulation deals directly with outcomes. Being powerful is getting what you want, but possible resistance is also built into the definition. This analysis leads us to a trivial truth. Under the capability approach probabilized into possible worlds analysis no-one has any power, for no single person nor any group can get anything done in every possible world: thus no-one has any political power. This trivial truth leads us to an important one. Every powerful actor is powerful because of the resources they bring to a bargain with other actors. Social power always depends upon a coalition of mutual or allied interests. Dictators rely upon many other people – their army, their police, their secret police, their cabinet and so on. All of these people, or some subset of them, could conspire and overthrow the dictator. Dictators survive by forming coalitions with others and stopping rival coalitions forming by sowing doubts in others' minds and turning potential partners against each other. The dictator offers positive and negative incentives to the others in order to gain their support and stop their challenge. In order to understand even the most obvious examples of social power, we need to understand the nature of coalition formation and the nature of bargaining. All political power is a form of reciprocal or bargaining power.

One may sooner be lucky than decisive, for then one gets what one wants without trying. One may sooner share the same interests with the powerful than be one of them. Individuals must make judgements about getting what they want by taking into account the interests they share with others, and judgements about power must be judgements about groups rather than individuals. What individuals take into account in these calculations are the resources that others could bring to bear against them in any social situation. The power of others is assessed solely in terms of their resources. These resources include both 'external' resources (e.g. money, legal rights, institutional authority) and 'internal' resources (e.g. physical strength, determination and persuasiveness). My account of power suggests that we need to study the resources of different groups in society, understand their preferences and model their relationship one to another.

The incentive approach to power

The power index approach places too much stress upon outcomes in its attempt to measure individual power. Harsanyi (1976a, b) tries to generalize the Shapley–Shubik power index by considering other resources that people bring to bargaining. Situated within a model of power and luck, his generalization can suggest the sorts of resources we should look for.

In Harsanyi's account of power, four sets of resources are important: (1) knowledge or information, (2) legitimate authority, (3) unconditional incentives to affect the interests of others, (4) conditional incentives to affect the interests of others. To these we can add (5) reputation, the importance of which we saw in some of the games in Chapter 1.

The first two seem straightforward. Having information is an important resource. Collecting information can be a costly business and supplying information often gives groups power over others. Governments rely upon their bureaucracies to supply them with the information necessary to produce and implement policy, and public bureaucracies rely upon professional groups, lobby groups and other organized groups and industries to supply much of that information. An important part of empowering citizens is not only a free press but an investigative one. One might think that collecting information is not a cost for journalists, since it is part and parcel of their job, but that job becomes easier if information is supplied. This is why industries, lobbies, political parties and governments employ public relations consultants to try to ensure that the press gets the information they want them to have. Sometimes the group's machine can be so effective as to rebound. When Shell wanted to dump the Brent Spar oilrig in the Atlantic Ocean, Greenpeace rallied public opinion against the company and the British government, forcing Shell, much to the government's dismay, to back down. Later the press felt that it had been manipulated by Greenpeace, through being invited on to their ship and to share in the excitement of the activists as they took on the oil company in mid-ocean. The press later believed that the oil company had some good environmental arguments for Atlantic dumping as the least damaging option, which were not effectively conveyed. The British Broadcasting Corporation brought in new guidelines for its journalists because of this case.

Legitimate authority is obviously a source of power. To have the force of law on one's side leads others to be more likely to comply. Authority also comes with knowledge. Professional groups often speak with authority on issues where they claim specialized knowledge. Thus doctors claim authority on health issues and teachers on educational affairs. When the Conservative government wished to introduce radical reforms in Britain's schools against the dominant wishes of the teaching lobby, it felt the need to break down the authority of the main teachers' lobbies. It attacked the power resources of the educational establishment, suggesting that teachers' unions were led by Marxists, that teaching policy in schools was driven by 'trendy' ideas created by teacher training in universities set up during the heyday of left-wing ideological hegemony, and that in the end parents know best. These tactics were typified by the Secretary of State for Education, who launched a slanderous assault upon a leading educationalist, describing him as a 'nutter' and claiming to 'fear for Birmingham with this madman let loose, wandering around the streets, frightening the children'.

Clearly this strategy was designed to undermine the legitimacy of teachers, their unions, teaching establishments and educationalists to speak with a professional voice on the care of children, their major power resource.

The third and fourth sets of resources are less obvious. They are the unconditional incentives to affect the interests of others, and the conditional incentives to affect the interests of others. One actor may provide another with a number of unconditional incentives that affect the second's calculations about his actions. They are unconditional in the sense that the second person bears the costs or receives the advantages no matter what he does. We saw this in Chapter 1 with the example of Lambeth Council deciding to bid for City Challenge money to set up Brixton City Challenge. The central government unconditionally changed the incentives facing local authorities, leading some to behave in ways in which they otherwise would not have. Conditional incentives are more straightforward. They are threats or offers, or throffers (a combination of threats and offers), which take the form, 'if you do x then I will do y'.

There is an important asymmetry between threats and offers: offers cost more when they succeed and threats cost more when they fail. Increasing an offer is likely to increase the probability of incurring the costs of success, whereas increasing a threat, as long as it remains credible, is likely to decrease the probability of incurring the costs of carrying it out. Keeping threats credible provides an important limitation on the degree of the threat. Schelling (1966: 35–6) argues that some threats are inherently credible, others inherently incredible. If there were no limitations on the credibility of threats, then it would always be worthwhile making the threat as great as possible.

One way of making a threat credible is to pre-commit oneself to carrying it out if the subject does not comply. Governments may pre-commit the state by passing legislation entailing heavy punishment, though even here if the punishment seems out of proportion to the crime juries may refuse to convict and judges try to find mitigating circumstances to reduce the penalty.[1] Attempts to pre-commit are another form of threat; for example, a trade union balloting its members for strike action if certain conditions are not met by management.

Making credible threats and carrying them out is very important to reputation. If one gets a reputation for making idle threats, then one loses all credibility. The business of the mafia is providing protection and Diego Gambetta has shown how important reputation is for the mafia and how cheap protection can be if one's reputation is good:

> By far the most striking feature of a mafioso's reputation is that it saves directly on production costs. Car manufacturers benefit from a good reputation, but they still have to produce cars. By contrast, a reputation for credible protection and protection itself tend to be one and the same thing. The more robust the reputation of a protection firm, the less the need to have recourse to the resources which support the reputation.
>
> (Gambetta 1993: 44)

The mafia gain their reputation through deliberate acts on their part, even if they do not in fact have the resources that those who fear them think they have. It is also possible to gain a fearsome reputation even if one does not intend it. Someone may be thought of as a mafioso simply because he wears dark sharp suits, sunglasses, never smiles and has been overheard denying the existence of the mafia. The 'rule of anticipated reactions' (Friedrich 1941) suggests that people will not press demands if they feel they will not get anywhere. This rule may work in favour of some groups either because they have acted to engender this reaction in others, or, though less often, through luck. Others believe that they will react unfavourably to some demand, and so do not make the demand, when in fact the response may be rather different.

Reputation is not only important to those who make threats, it is also important to those who may suffer them. We cannot simply measure the value to B of A's threat to her. If B acts to maximize her expected utility, then the action she should choose in the absence of A's threat will have a higher utility than the action to which she is coerced. If t_1 is the measure of the disutility to B of the sanction A threatens, then the threat will be successful if $t_1 > u_1 - u_2$, where u_1 is the utility to B of carrying out her preferred course of action without the threat, and u_2 of carrying out the coerced action. The difference $u_1 - u_2$ that A can make to B's welfare is the measure of A's power. In fact A does not necessarily have that much power. In the same way that one may wish to develop a reputation for toughness in a repeated Chicken game, one may find it advantageous to refuse to comply with threats in order to develop a reputation for stubbornness. There will be costs to A of carrying out his threat and thus he will want to threaten those who are most likely to comply. Thus there are incentives to B to develop a reputation as someone who does not comply with threats.

Reputation is a key element in bargaining and game theory. It depends on players having incomplete and imperfect information. If players had complete and perfect information, there would be no room for reputation, for there would be no room for players to pretend they were anything other than what they are. Thus the importance of information arises from asymmetry in information. It shows that we cannot simply read off actors' power from their resources – the so-called 'vehicle fallacy' (Morriss 1987: 18) which equates power with its vehicle – and shows that determinate game-theoretic accounts are impossible. It also demonstrates, as we saw in the repeated Battle of the Sexes game, that individuals' preferences and their power can be formed by the way they play the game, rather than the game being played by them given their preferences and resources. We should also note that stubbornness can apply to offers as well as threats, and indeed to Harsanyi's first three resource categories (Dowding 1991: 77–9).

Despite this limitation on a resource-based account of power, the best place to start studying the power of groups in society is to look at their resources, modelled in the context of their luck and given sets of imputed preferences. What sort of resources should we look for? How should we go about studying them?

A method for studying power

When studying power in society, the political scientist will use various different sources of information. First she should have a clear idea of what she is looking for. We must begin with a model of the area (say power in a city). This model will impute certain relationships between the actors and assume what interests each actor has. The modellist has to think very carefully about which actors to include in the model. It is not enough, for example, merely to think about actors who live in the locale, for some important relationships will extend far beyond the city boundaries. A simple model might look like that shown in Figure 3.1.

Figure 3.1 consists of some of the major actors in the power structure of an imagined city. Each box represents a single actor. At the centre we have the elected city council with a separate box for

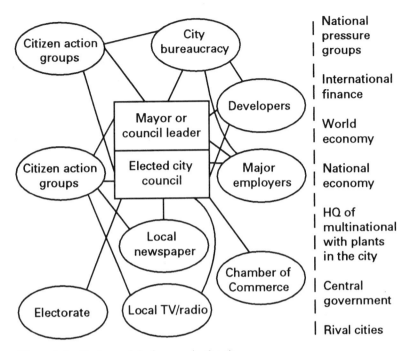

National pressure groups

International finance

World economy

National economy

HQ of multinational with plants in the city

Central government

Rival cities

Figure 3.1 Basic model of power in the city.

the council leadership, which in many US and European cities will be the mayor and in Britain and other European cities will be the council leader. The city bureaucracy is another actor, with citizen and pressure groups on one side, local developers, major employers and the chamber of commerce on the other. The local newspaper, television or radio may also be key actors. Each actor is standing alone in the figure, but a whole series of lines drawn between the boxes represents different types of relationships. Obviously, the elected council and mayor require the support of the majority of the electorate, so a line needs to be drawn there. The interests of the electorate will be affected by the actions of the council, so another line can be drawn between these two boxes. Similarly, decisions made by the major employers affect the local citizenry, and those employers will keep a close eye on the actions of the council, lobbying when necessary. Developers need the support of the council so they will also lobby, and countervailing forces may be felt by the council through the citizen action groups. The figure has two boxes for citizen action groups because some may be in conflict with others, for example over the siting of a sports stadium. The council looks to the bureaucracy for policy initiatives as well as policy implementation. The lobbying groups will understand that the bureaucracy is just as important to their plans as the elected politicians, so will lobby the bureaucracy just as much if not more than the council. The bureaucracy also needs the support of other groups. It may require technical information from the employer groups such as the Chamber of Commerce, information from the citizen action groups, and to some extent the support of the electorate for policy implementation. The local newspaper may also be important. It will act as a battleground for competing ideas about the policies of the city. The groups will try to get their views put forward in the newspaper, which may also campaign independently. The ownership of the newspaper and the range of its readership is thus also important. Outside the city we have national pressure groups who may be interested in given policy initiatives in this city. International finance will be involved if large loans are required for major developments. The world economic situation will affect what the actors in this city will believe is possible and thus constitutes a major structural constraint on their activities. Other decisions in cities across the world may affect what happens in this city. One of the major employers may have a head office in another country. Decisions made there will affect the local economy. Other multinationals may be opening new plants or offices and their decisions about where to locate will affect this city. Other cities may be competing for the location of new plants or more generally for trade, and their decisions affect this city. Thus if one city decides to promote growth through local tax incentives, local business and developers may press the council to do the same in this city.

Quite where the lines are drawn, and whether they represent cooperation or conflict, will depend upon the exact nature of the local economy, the interests of each of the actors and the politics of the city. Each of the unitary actors in the figure can be broken down. For example, the 'bureaucracy' consists of the local police, social welfare officers, fire service, education, tax service and both the lower and higher levels of those services. How the bureaucracy is organized – whether it is simple line bureaucracy organized hierarchically or separate agencies with few formal links – will affect its role. The power of the elected leaders of cities varies enormously, some having many discretionary powers, some having few. In many cities, the unelected chief executives of the bureaucracy will have more discretionary powers than the elected leader, in others not.

The electorate might be considered as a single actor for some issues, or as several for others, where for example there is racial tension between different parts of the community. However, what Figure 3.1 presents is a simple model that may be described as a network diagram. Before empirical analysis, but based upon casual acquaintance with the city under study, the analyist can draw such a model. It may be very different for different policy areas. For example, city action groups may operate in some policy areas but be absent from others. Some issues are controversial, others more routine but no less important, waste disposal for example (though even this, as all other policy areas, can erupt into conflict). The simple model will suggest to the researcher where to look for relationships, and who should be approached. After initial analysis, the models may be redrawn. For example, we may begin by thinking that the mayor will be at the centre of the policy network, but later find him marginalized and the chief executive and a local developer at the centre. But how do we come to modify our figures, decide who is most powerful, and discover the relationships which exist? There are many techniques.

The researcher will use both primary and secondary sources of information, quantitative and qualitative information. She will collect data on the personnel and budgets of the major actors. She will interview key actors (using semi-structured interviewing, supported perhaps by questionnaire-based analysis), asking them about the power resources they feel they and others have. She will try to discover actors' reputations by asking others about them, and discover how those reputations were engendered by asking them how they go about their job. She will not necessarily believe all she is told, but will cross-refer answers to try to get a picture of the actual situation. She will also try to analyse quantitatively the local and national media to the view of an omnivorous reader of the press. This is now relatively easy given the ready availability of on-line sources of press coverage. Thus she can discover the limits of what informed citizens could know, and gain some idea of the power structure as seen by one key player. Though obviously many key actors try to keep what they are doing out of the view of the media. All of this information will be fed into a model of the power structure, which (a) tries to develop a picture of the preferences and interests of the main actors, (b) studies the resources they have to use in the power arena, (c) sees the coalitions which develop which enhance the power of actors, (d) looks at those coalitions to see if others benefit as a by-product and thus get what they want through luck, and (e) compares the situation in this city now with how it was, how other cities are and how it might be, to see if the city as a whole can act to get a relatively large or small amount of things done. Some structures enable actors to carry through ideas, other structures may overall impede actors. I shall begin by considering the five sets of power resources that actors may have and how these enter into the model as illustrated by Figure 3.1.

Knowledge or information

An old maxim, 'knowledge is power', is an important one. Having information is important not only for knowing what it is that you want to do, for understanding your own interests, it is also something that can be traded. Information is one of the major sources of power for the bureaucracy, as Weber (1978: 1417–18) recognized:

> Apart from being rooted in the administrative division of labour, the power of all bureaucrats rests upon knowledge of two kinds: First, technical know-how in the widest sense of the word acquired through specialized training . . . However, expertise alone does not explain the power of the bureaucracy. In addition, the bureaucrat has official information, which is available through administrative channels and which provides him with the facts on which he can base his actions. Only he who can get access to these facts independently of the officials' good will can effectively supervise the administration . . . the bureaucracy's supreme power instrument is the transformation of official information into classified material by means of the notorious concept of the 'official secret'. In the last analysis, this is merely a means of protecting the administration against supervision.[2]

Bureaucrats obtain their information from various sources and the information they gain from pressure lobbies, industry, trade unions and citizen groups is important. Ensuring that this information is secret, and procedures exist for keeping their policy discussions from public scrutiny, enables bureaucracies to carry more weight.

The information and expertise that groups have are important.

Many groups, because of specialist knowledge, can claim to speak authoritatively on certain issues. Certainly this is a major power resource for professional groups which their opponents may feel the need to attack in conflict situations, as we saw with central government and the educational establishment in Britain in the late 1980s and early 1990s. Discovering which sources of information are most trusted by bureaucrats and policy-makers is important in discovering a hidden power structure. How attitudes change over time can also be explained through the diffusion of knowledge from specialists through the bureaucracy and public. The growing public and bureaucratic concern with the environment is such an example of this power over time, which has led Paul Sabatier and others to stress the importance of looking at policy over many years (Sabatier and Jenkins-Smith 1993). They also stress how important the process of learning is. Advocacy coalitions may develop through groups which at first seem antagonistic, but over time come to realize that through compromise and understanding they can form policy proposals which suit both sides; or groups may come to realize through information and persuasion that their interests are not threatened by some proposal, or that their interests were not what they were thought to be. Knowledge or information is a major source of power both for defending and promoting one's interests, and for understanding what those interests are.

Because information is a source of power, so too is secrecy. Actors often do not want others to know what their true interests are, with whom they are bargaining and for what. Much of the lobbying goes on behind closed doors. Seeing lobbies give evidence on TV before congressional committees or select committees in the House of Commons is merely the public face of lobbying. Far more occurs through telephone conversations, by mail, through informal discusssions at parties, and through formal and informal meetings (ones with and without minutes being taken). Such meetings take place between most of the groups in Figure 3.1 at one time or another. When some groups feel excluded from this informational and lobbying exchange, they may try to open out the system by creating wider dissemination of the issues in a public airing. Here the mass media are very important. Some groups will plan press campaigns for months to try to seize the agenda at a given moment, or they may realize that a press campaign is necessary because they cannot get their views across in any other way. A rule of thumb is that those groups which feel the need to go public are the ones who are weakest. The really strong actors do not need the weight of public opinion or public scrutiny, for they already have the inside track.

Legitimate authority

Expert knowledge gives some groups the ability to speak with authority. Their spokespeople will be asked to comment in the media, will be sought out for advice and can be important allies for others in policy battles. But actors may also be *in* authority as well as *an* authority. They may have a more direct source of power through being able to give authoritative commands to other actors. Many people find themselves in this position. Each property owner has the legitimate authority to direct others over their use of that property. Each person in a direct line of command in a hierarchy has the authority to order those below them to act in certain ways, and those below them have the authority to refuse if those commands go beyond the rights their superior has to expect. In political situations, the most obvious use of legitimate authority is for law-makers to make laws or regulations for others to follow. These may directly command others or shape their interests, as changing the rules over government grants for development changed the behaviour of Lambeth councillors (see Chapter 1). Authority is legitimate to the extent that it is law-bound and others accept that it is legitimate. Legal theorists usually explain this mixed notion of force and acceptance as acting for 'content-independent' reasons (see Green 1988: 36–54; see also Friedman 1973; Hart 1982; Raz 1986). I do what you say, not because what you say is what I think is right, but because I think it right that what you say is the right thing to do. My reasons for carrying out those actions are independent of the content of those actions. However, my acceptance of your authority may be undermined if you continually order me to carry out actions which I think are wrong, or which continue to have bad consequences. I will trust you, but only so far. Once I start to be unwilling, then authority breaks down into a cruder form of power, of threats and offers.

Conditional incentives to affect others

Conditional incentives to affect others come in the form of threats, offers and a mixture of threats and offers usually called 'throffers'.

Most contractual relations are a form of promise. One party offers to supply the other with a certain set of goods, if the other supplies another set of goods such as money. Money is an obvious source of power, and budgetary analysis of the various organizations within a community to see where the money comes from, and what it is spent on, gives an idea of the nature of power dependency that different groups have to one another. Many groups depend for their survival on the flow of money through their budgets, and what they choose to spend their money on helps to reveal what that group's preferences are. Of course, much of the monetary flow, particularly of public organizations, is statutory. The organization is mandated to spend money on different sets of things by higher authorities, or it has agreed to spend so much on certain sorts of services in a contract with, say, the electorate. What groups choose to spend the discretionary parts of their budgets on can reveal preferences of the moment.

Most political actors are engaged in a constant set of negotiations over policy. Semi-structured interviewing will reveal the content of those negotiations and the relative powers of the different actors as well as the sources of those powers. Personalities can count for a lot in such face-to-face negotiations, as can allegiances which extend beyond the policy under negotiation. In Britain during the 1980s, a number of leading local politicians in the London borough of Wandsworth had close personal and ideological links with the Prime Minister, Margaret Thatcher. They suggested many policy initiatives and agreed to pilot various central government initiatives at the local level. These close links enabled the council to negotiate over a series of issues in which they were interested, including educational policy, housing policy and initiatives on crime. But government is complex, and while Wandsworth Council enjoyed close links through ministers, their relationship with senior civil servants was not always so close and in certain policy areas they enjoyed poor relations. For example, Wandsworth wanted to take over control of certain aspects of health policy from the local heath authority controlled by the Department of Health. Here Wandsworth came into direct conflict with central government and their close relationship in other policy areas did not help them at all. Different policy areas often have very different working practices and different sets of relations with actors. Different policy communities are often shielded almost completely from others (Jordan

and Richardson 1987a, b; Rhodes 1988; Petracca 1992; Rhodes and
Marsh 1992; Heinz *et al.* 1993).

In some ways, the bargaining process of conditional incentives is
the easiest part of the power structure to study. Bargaining can take
many forms. It can take place in public through the media. Often
groups will begin with a media campaign to highlight the issues.
Formal and informal meetings take place. Each side may try to
make offers or threats with whatever resources they have available:
money, labour, information or votes. Governments can sometimes
fail to understand that forcing a policy initiative will only be
successful if those who are supposed to implement that policy agree
with it. Many policy initiatives in, for example, health care or
education fail if the professional groups which have to implement
them believe them to be unworkable.

Unconditional incentives to affect others

The ability to structure others' choice situations is a major power
resource. In order to understand this aspect of power in society, it is
not enough to ask people what they want and how they go about
getting what they want. We need to model the choice situations of
each actor, and see how the scope of different decisions and actions
affects the other actors in the policy arena. Understanding the
unconditional incentives which affect others is as much a theoretical
as an empirical exercise. It concerns changing the environment of
actors. It is a structural alteration in their decision situation which
not only changes their behaviour given fixed preferences but may
even change what those preferences are. We have seen several
examples of this earlier in the book and we shall examine other
examples later when we look at luck and systematic luck, so we shall
leave this important aspect of the power structure aside for the
moment.

Reputation

As we saw above, reputation is now recognized as a key power
resource in bargaining theory. How do we examine it in the field?
Reputation is an extremely slippery concept to assess empirically.
Actors may enjoy different reputations among different sets of
people, and may indeed try to engender those different sets of

reputations. Some people may have a reputation in the media of being powerful which is not verified through insider interviews, yet their media reputation will still be a source of power. Others may be virtually unknown in the media yet be described as very powerful by insiders. Reputation can be approached with a three-fold process.

First is the model itself, in which actors are located in a series of relations and assumptions are generated (and later checked and modified against the evidence) about their intentions and interests and their various power resources. Examining the actions of players in a bargaining game allows us to infer reputation from the interactions, and also to infer whether or not actors are attempting to signal to others how they will treat them in the future – in other words, how they are trying to gain a reputation in different fields.

Secondly, their reputation is surmised through elite questioning, much like the 'reputational' approach of Hunter (1963) and others. Here actors can be asked to draw up lists of policy influentials in their fields, and these lists cross-checked against one another. The method of 'triangulation' can also be adopted (see Denzin 1978; Jick 1979). Here, person x is asked about the relationship between y and z. For example, the director of housing in a local council might be asked about the relationship between the major housing association in their jurisdiction and the Department of Environment (which is the main ministry dealing with local government and housing policy). Someone from the housing association can then be asked about their relationship with the Department of Environment, the director of housing of the local council and about the relationship between the director of housing and the Department of Environment, and someone from the Department of Environment can be asked about their relations with the housing association, the director of housing and about what they think the relationship between housing director and the housing asociation are. Triangulation is usually used to cross-check and verify claims made by different actors about the power structure. But it is also revealing for reputational research. For example, the director of housing may believe that the Department of Environment and the housing association have a close working relationship and feel excluded. He may therefore negotiate more carefully with the housing association because he does not wish to antagonize the Department of Environment, which has a certain amount of authority over the local council and is in an important monetary relationship providing funds for local councils. However, the researcher may discover that the Department and the housing association do not enjoy the relationship imputed to them; yet, simply because it is imputed, the housing association has greater power *vis à vis* the housing department of the local council than its other resources would suggest. Triangulation is thus an important method of discovering the reputation of actors within their policy domain and whether that reputation is based on reality or not. Either way, however, reputation is an important power resource.

Thirdly, the reputation of actors can be examined through the eyes of the media. Many media databases now exist. In the USA, newspapers are on-line through Nexis; in Britain, FTProfile contains the major broadsheet and some tabloid national newspapers plus London's *Evening Standard*; Reuters is on Textline and *Keesing's Contemporary Archives* may be consulted through CDRom. Similar databases exist in other countries. This enables the researcher to examine the depth and scope of press coverage of major actors. The scale of any actor's public reputation can be mapped quantitatively in the scope and character of press coverage. A media reputational score for each actor may be generated in terms of the number of times different people are mentioned in the press, with whom they are mentioned and whether the coverage is positive or negative. This media coverage may then be used to compare and contrast with the reputation revealed through elite interviewing of the policy insiders who may also be asked directly or indirectly whether they court media publicity or shun it.

Reputation may be deliberately engendered or gained through luck and the analysis through behaviour, elite questioning and media analysis is extremely complex. Figure 3.2 represents these relations diagrammatically. There are three sorts of reputation in Figure 3.2. Reputation I is reputation as a bargaining resource. It is the reputation in which we are interested in our modelling of the power structure. It has two parts, I(i) the deliberate and strategic use of reputation to gain bargaining advantages, and I(ii) reputation gained by the actor without any intention. Both may be inspected directly through behaviour of the actor, and the reactions of other actors; they may also be examined through elite interviewing and through media analysis. Other elites and the media may enhance an actor's reputation $(+)$ or may diminish that reputation $(-)$. The actors themselves may try to enhance their reputation through their

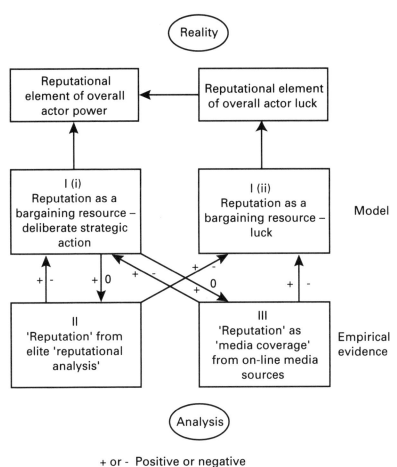

Figure 3.2 Types of reputations and their relationships.

behaviour with other actors or the media (+), or they may try to avoid appearing in newspapers, or avoid conflict with other elites by keeping a low profile (0). It can be seen therefore that we borrow 'reputation' from economics, seeing it as a power resource, or a source of luck. Reputation I may be examined by a model-driven direct inspection of behaviour. Reputation II may be examined through elite interviewing generating lists of notables, understanding reputations through the triangulation method. Reputation III can be generalized by combing any relevant media database to generate a list of their media scores. This gives a complete analysis of reputation.

Notes

1 See Tsebelis (1990; 1991) and Bianco and Tsebelis (1990) for some counterintuitive ideas about the relationship between crime and punishment.
2 Following David Beetham's (1985: 74) translation, I have changed the original 'service secret' to the more familiar 'official secret'.

4

Systematic Luck

Outcome power is the ability to get what you want. Looking at who benefits provides us with some evidence of power. It is a mistake just to read back from who benefits to power, since those who benefit may simply be lucky. However, the distribution of luck in society is not mere happenstance. There are reasons why some groups in society are able to get what they desire without having to act, but rather have their wishes supplied by others as a by-product of the latter's actions. Lack of outcome power may well be the result of the hostile application of the social power of others, but it may not be. The powerless may be impersonally oppressed by the logic of situations as well as by the directed social power of others.

Some groups of people are lucky: they get what they want from society without having to act. Some groups are systematically lucky: they get what they want without having to act because of the way society is structured. It may seem odd to think that luck can be systematic, but it denotes the fact that people may get what they want without trying and this property attaches to certain locations within the social and institutional structure. Luck in this sense is closer to fortune or destiny than to simple chance. Being given what you want all the time is not the same as acting to get what you want all the time. There is an important disjunction between getting what you want and outcome power, even when we expect that certain types of people get what they want without trying. Political science tends to denote people by their social locations (they are capitalists, or developers, or bureaucrats, or party activists) – they are not denoted by their personal identities. Actors denoted by their social location have powers based upon their social resources, and they also have luck based upon their social location. In this chapter, we will look at systematic luck in two contexts: first, systematic luck at the national state level through neo-marxist and state-autonomy models; secondly, systematic luck at the local level reflected in the literature in urban politics concerning the 'growth machine' and regime-based politics.

The systematic luck of capitalists

Adam Przeworski (1986; cf. Przeworski and Sprague 1985) suggests a model which can be used to illustrate the nature of systematic luck in the capitalist state. We do not have to agree with all the elements of Przeworski's model to see how systematic luck may operate in a weaker form. He argues that the capitalist democratic system, with its regular cycle of elections, constrains any democratic socialist party from changing the economy from a capitalist mode of production to a socialist one. In other words, large-scale redistribution of property rights in a democratic capitalist system is not possible. His model works even if (1) a socialist economy is in the material interests of the working classes, (2) the working classes are in the majority, (3) all classes vote for the party which is in their material interests, because (4) the shift from a capitalist system to a socialist one will be costly, and (5) the time-frame of those dislocational costs is greater than the electoral cycle. With these assumptions, Przeworski shows that the electoral cycle in a capitalist democracy may constrain socialist parties from bringing about socialism.

In Figure 4.1, $s-s_1$ is the material well-being of the majority working class under socialism, $c-c_1$ the material well-being of the majority working class under capitalism. Under the above five assumptions, the working class would sooner be under socialism. However, if they live in a capitalist society at time t_1 and then try to move to socialism, they will be worse off until time t_3, reaching their lowest point at time t_2, when they will be much worse off than if they had stayed under capitalism. Only after t_3 do things get better and they can eventually reach the higher levels of welfare available for them under socialism at time t_4. The valley of transition that they must undergo to get to socialism may seem too great for workers to want to traverse it. Revolution brings costs, and individuals may not wish to pay those costs even if there are expected rewards at the end. What matters is the length of time between t_1 and t_4.

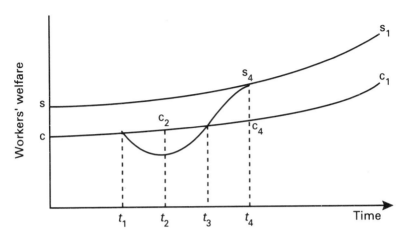

Figure 4.1 The valley of transition.
Source: modified from Przenorski (1986: 177)

We can see that even under democracy the majority working class may not vote for a party that tries to traverse the valley. Downs (1957) assumes that political parties are coalitions of individuals sharing certain views about policy. As such, coalition parties do not have a single preference ordering; rather, their official policies are compromises between the various factions, compromises which are largely driven by electoral considerations. The electorate's perception of the competence of each party is largely derived from how well it manages to run the country when in power. If moving from a capitalist to a socialist economy requires traversing the valley, then this course will only appeal to those who will gain in the long run. In Przeworski's argument, that is the majority working class. But they will only vote for a party undergoing that journey if they can see the benefits of such a transformation. If the time between t_1 and t_4 is, say, 30 years, but the electoral cycle is only 4–5 years, we can appreciate that a social democratic party may have difficulties in trying to be a revolutionary one.

This stark example shows how capitalists may be systematically lucky. If a socialist party, one that would like to change the nature of property rights, cannot afford to try to do so because it will lead to electoral failure, then capitalists can rest assured that their position in society is not under threat. The question for democratic parties is how to run the economy in such a way that it is successful, and that means running it in a manner in which capitalism thrives. As the leader of Britain's social democratic Labour Party once stated, the role for Labour is to run capitalism better than the Tories.

Capital constraints are systematic in the sense that they are non-random: they depend upon a relatively enduring set of relations between a set of actors understood in terms of the functional roles they occupy in society and in the economy. The system of relations is such that no single actor is necessary or sufficient for the continuance of the system, and if one or more actors fail to fulfil their roles there are strong incentives for others to take their place.

The constraints upon the action of the state – at national, federal and local levels – exist because of the type of economy under which elected state officials act. Politicians' actions are modified by economic factors because they face election and re-election. They will not be re-elected if the economy plunges into recession, so they must ensure that their policies help the economy – which means helping the interests of capital. This does not itself make capital powerful. Rather, it is lucky, for capital does not set the constraints upon what is feasible; it simply benefits from that which is (Elster 1988: 213). Elster imagines a situation where the government wishes to maximize tax revenue, which is a function of the rate of taxation. If the tax rate is 0, then revenue is 0; if the tax rate is 100, then revenue is 0, for no taxable activity will occur. Where the optimal rate of taxation occurs is determined by the position of the Laffer curve and where this lies is an empirical matter over which government and no individual capitalist has any control. If it is high, then capitalists are unlucky; if it is low, then they are lucky. Capitalists are just lucky that what is in the interests of the government is also, by and large, in their interests as well. They have no need to intervene partly because they are lucky, and partly because the politicians may be afraid to act in ways contrary to the interests of business lest businessmen do intervene. This highlights power of the rule of anticipated reactions, which may demonstrate either luck or power.

However, capitalists are not *merely* lucky. First, this luck is systematic. They have it because of the function they systematically perform in the economy. Secondly, collectively they exert some control over where the Laffer curve lies. They do not have to act collectively in order to utilize that collective power, for they collectively have that power even though they act individually. Acting collectively may utilize that power most effectively, but there is little evidence to suggest that capitalists have done so.

Business power

Saying that business is systematically lucky does not mean that it is not also powerful. The state may pursue policies which are broadly in the interests of business, but that does not mean that it always does so, nor that there are not conflicts between industries and between firms within industries. Business regularly intervenes in the policy process and does so from a position of privilege, not only because its interests are often those of elected politicians, but also because of the close relationship between capital and government through their institutional links and the close relationship through personal, family and social class ties. There is much evidence that people from similar social backgrounds take up important bureaucratic state roles (in both local communities and national government) and within business (Mills 1956; Domhoff 1983; Ellis 1995; Hutton 1996). This increases the outcome power of business, eased also by the structural relationships illustrated by Przeworski's model (cf. Lindblom 1977; Grant 1987), which systematically makes them lucky.

Different sectors of the business lobby compete with one another. Competition between firms within industries and between industries gives rise to sectoral cleavages in the clamour for government attention. One of the largest cleavages is the conflict between finance capital and productive capital, and within the latter group small business and large-scale business often have very different interests. The distinction between finance capital and productive capital has been recognized as very important, particularly by British commentators who have often viewed it as part and parcel of Britain's decline (e.g. Coates 1984). The distinction between the two is not as clear-cut as sometimes imagined, and certainly Britain is not that different from other nations. Productive firms have often tied up much of their monetary assets in financial deals which have had little to do with production and have beome even more involved in finance as 'takeover fever' has taken over. The development of professional corporate treasurers within large firms is one aspect of this convergence. Directors of companies transcend the finance–production divide as multiple directorships multiply. However, this interlocking of the two does not mean that the interests of finance and production are converging. Grant (1987: 79) is correct in his assertion that 'financiers and industrialists seem to recognize that what unites them is more important than what divides them'. What unites them is making money; what divides them is how they go about that process.

The removal of financial controls across the world has made the role of international financiers easier and this has led productive capital to become more involved with finance as a result. But this does not mean that the interests of the two are becoming closer. What is happening is that finance is taking over from production. In the present environment, it is the fitter genotype. As portfolio diversification of investors increases, and the nature of investors moves more to corporations than individual people, the less bothered investment capital is about the productive strength of any given individual firm. What matters is which firm is doing well now, and if it does badly soon, investment can easily be shifted. Risk is spread by portfolio diversification, which means that less care needs to be taken by investors when considering the running of the productive firms into which they invest (Schondhart-Bailey and Bailey 1995). This radically affects the interests of everyone in the community as a by-product of changes made by government in the interests of financiers and finance capitalists. We can see this argument reappearing in miniature with the growth machine in local politics.

Systematic luck and the growth machine

Two theoretical developments dominate the study of urban politics: the growth-machine model (Molotch 1976, 1979, 1990; Domhoff 1983, 1986; Harding 1991, 1994, 1995; Logan and Molotch 1984, 1987; Molotch and Vicari 1988; Cox and Mair 1989; Molotch and Logan 1990) and the idea of local regimes (Stone 1989, 1993; Horan 1991; Jones and Bachelor 1993; Orr and Stoker 1994; Stoker and Mossberger 1994; Stoker 1995). The first is a variant of elite theory, the second a more complex model of power relations. Both illustrate the relationship between power and systematic luck. I will look at each in turn, showing how the second develops out of and is broader than the first, but also demonstrating that regime theory, without a model of power and luck, is descriptive rather than explanatory.

Modern elite theory in urban politics was first rigorously applied in the 1950s by Hunter (1963) in his study of 'Regional City' (Atlanta). He employed reputational analysis, beginning by identifying community influentials whom he thought likely to be powerful. A panel then ranked these influentials, the top forty of whom were interviewed to discover whom they thought were the most powerful. With the exception of the mayor, almost all of the top influentials were businessmen and few would be known to the ordinary citizens of Atlanta. Importantly for Stone's (1989) later study of Atlanta, Hunter created a separate list of black influentials derived from a black panel, which constituted 'a sub-power grouping of considerable significance which could not be overlooked, particularly since many of the issues suggested to the field investigator by white power personnel revolved around Negro–white relations' (Hunter 1963: 263).

Three general criticisms were levelled at Hunter by critics (see Harding 1995). First, his method assumed a single elite; secondly, he concentrated on individuals rather than positions in the social structure; and thirdly, that a reputation for power had to be backed up by evidence that they actually wielded power.

The first criticism is unfounded since Hunter's method could have found evidence of competing elites, as indeed the evidence for a black sub-elite demonstrates. What is true is that he concentrates upon development issues, and he may have found different networks of policy actors in different policy domains. However, development has been found to be one – if not the key – issue in virtually all studies of urban communities. Hunter's reputational analysis came in for most criticism, but as we have seen reputation is itself a source of power, and may be used by means of the rule of anticipated reactions even if a person does little overtly to wield power. Evidence of activity other than mere reputation *is* required in order to substantiate claims about a power elite. While Hunter did concentrate upon individuals, the fact that they tended to occupy certain positions in the social structure is suggestive of a positional account of power, and it is this that the growth-machine model builds upon. Not all the potency of the growth-machine model is built upon power, however; systematic luck plays an important part, again weakening the third criticism of Hunter's analysis.

The growth-machine model concentrates upon the shared interests of certain groups within the social structure around the political economy of place. The importance of the fixed capital of land in communities is paramount, for all property-owners share an interest in seeing land values rise. Local economic growth and new development constitute an important source of elevation. The growth-machine model supposes that local power is structured around land-based interests. A common bonding for both home-owners and capitalists or *rentiers* is creating the conditions for attracting outside investment. Local government will find itself promoting development and needing to secure the backing of major local and national developers. This power is structured around elite figures who intertwine among boards of directors of local companies and banks and will often appear on the boards of public and quasi-public organizations.

Logan and Molotch (1984, 1987) may be placed squarely in the elite tradition, for they argue that the decision-making system works to the advantage of the developers and against those of the local citizens. For while growth may appear to be good for all, its advantages are not distributed equally. The fact that the growth machine favours exchange values over use values does not produce the local growth that will provide jobs, and the jobs that are provided will not necessarily go to local people. Finance is favoured over production, production over housing, and high-value housing over low-value housing. Thus the development of slum areas will not necessarily bring any benefits to slum-dwellers, while the costs of development are likely to be endured by the poorest groups. Low-income communities and marginal local businesses are often physically displaced by new development and find themselves competing with new residents and commuters from outside the central city area. Local economic growth is not necessarily a positive-sum game. Even where local economic growth is positive-sum it is not always a Pareto-improvement. While there may be overall gains to the community in the sense that the gainers gain more than the losers, there may well be losers and these may be the poorest members of the community. Competition between cities for growth potential may lead to overall loss. Local elected officials usually see any employment opportunity as beneficial and tend to back local growth strategies in ways which shape the incentives of local people in favour of development. If one area aggressively favours local growth with supply-side incentives for business to locate there, another finds its local employment prospects declining. Thus all localities are forced to devise incentives in the form of subsidies, tax breaks or infrastructural reform for business. Each community finds itself in a Prisoners' Dilemma or Chicken game against all other communities, in which there may be no nation-wide increase in growth, just a transfer of resources from the public purse to business. The fact that these inter-community Prisoners' Dilemmas exist helps to structure the interests of the local communities towards development in their own areas. While business may encourage this process, as the growth machine argues, the interests are structured thus by the fact of community competition, and not necessarily by the deliberate actions of any people. In fact, local growth is not simply zero-sum, though it is doubtful whether local growth strategies add to the positive elements of that sum. In recent years, more communities have come to recognize that growth is not necessarily in their interests and anti-growth or 'managed growth' coalitions have developed. These latter coalitions try to wrest control from the developers and manage development in ways which more clearly benefit the local community (Schneider *et al.* 1995: ch. 7).

The interest side of the growth-machine model is important. Logan and Molotch argue that historically growth is rarely opposed in major cities. Conflict concerns the exact nature of development and where it is to be placed. In part, the emphasis upon development is seen as ideological. Molotch (1976: 320) describes employment as the 'key ideological prop for the growth machine', but it is also the key welfare prop for most people. What is important is whether the nature of local growth is the best way of promoting welfare for local people. At most the growth-machine model provides evidence for the outcome power of landed, capitalist and business interests, but it does not demonstrate the degree of power that they often assume. While businesspeople may be the prime movers, they still need elected and non-elected officials, and when local people do oppose development the growth machine may fail. The growth machine is not using social power if it acts with the acquiescence of the majority of the local population. The growth-machine writers have not demonstrated that these elites are sufficiently powerful to achieve development despite opposition. Below we shall look at some examples where anti-growth coalitions have succeeded. First, however, let us consider luck.

One of the problems for the growth-machine model is that it tries to demonstrate the power of local growth elites when it should demonstrate their systematic luck. Local growth may be supported by most of the community and the battle is over the nature of that growth. We can thus split growth into two games: a positive-sum game over the growth possibilities, and a zero-sum game over where that development is to occur. The first game is positive-sum. Developers and landed interests gain even more through growth than does the local community, but if local jobs are created or secured, then many in the local community will gain. If developers agree to provide some low-cost housing as a result of bargaining with local politicians for building rights, then many local people may gain more directly. In so far as the developers are able to gain because others gain too, they are pushing at an open door. To that extent they are lucky: what is in their interests is in others' interests too. This is an important aspect of the power structure. In a capitalist society, capitalists are systematically lucky because the welfare of everyone is dependent upon the state of the economy and capitalism is the motor of the economy. We need to say more about this.

Anti-growth coalitions

The growth machine does not always get its way. The Prisoners' Dilemma suggests that if cities do not encourage growth, then in a competitive market they will decline. It is therefore irrational for cities not to help growth coalitions. However, many local communities do not promote growth. Does this make them irrational? The answer is 'no', because growth is not in the interests of everyone in the community and people can get together to fight it. Studies linking social characteristics with anti-growth coalitions have failed to find a consistent relationship between anti-growth and pro-growth (for example, middle-class areas are more likely to be anti-growth) but one finding is clear: 'Organized groups play a distinct role in fostering citizen concern and leadership respon-siveness concerning growth-related policies' (Clark and Goetz 1994: 109, emphasis removed). Where the growth machine suggests an almost inevitable dominance of business elites, the anti-growth coalitions which have formed and forced managed growth strategies in many areas show that pluralistic power is alive and kicking in at least some communities. We need to look at this local pluralism, and also see why Clark and Goetz are wrong to call it 'the anti-growth *machine*'.

We have seen how developers are systematically lucky in the sense that what is in their interests tends to be in the interests of everyone else. Communities thrive on good housing, good shops and other services and employment opportunities. These are just the things that developers promise. But not all development is in everyone's interests, which is why controlled-growth public entrepreneurs can step in to try to manage growth in the interests of the community. A community which already feels comfortable with its housing, amenities and employment opportunities may not desire development at all. The developers' promise may just be the promise to ruin the natural environment as far as such communities are concerned. Clark and Goetz's study of 179 cities showed that a quarter had anti-growth coalitions fighting development. In their quantitative study, they showed that anti-growth coalitions were more likely to emerge in cities with more college graduates, higher income levels, greater numbers of professionals and technicians, higher Sierra Club membership (showing an interest in environmental issues), fewer black residents, and 'higher scores in the New Fiscal Populism index' (Clark and Goetz 1994: 126). This latter is an index of the use of innovative strategies, particularly productivity-improvement strategies and more sophisticated management practices (Clark and Fergusen 1983). This seems to show that those communities which are better off and with more stable employment and therefore less worried about the threat of unemployment and competition from other places are much more likely to feel that development is not in their interests and to fight it. A concern with the environment and less class-dominated politics (perhaps revealed by the New Fiscal Populism index) are also more likely to lead to anti-growth coalitions. Of course, not all communities which do not want growth have anti-growth coalitions; some may not need them if there are fewer demands for development or the city managers are managing growth themselves. Schneider *et al.* (1995) have demonstrated how important public entrepreneurs can be in mitigating the effects of the growth machine and Clark and Goetz (1994: 136) conclude:

> Anti-growth policy patterns differ in two contexts. In the first, citizens mobilize against the nonresponsiveness of local officials;

groups then significantly affect policy outcomes. In other contexts,
elected officials come to office supporting a political culture of
environmentalism and social liberalism. One causal step back, of
course, they often reached office and chose these growth-limiting
policies with encouragement from active organized groups.

In a democracy, organized interests lobbying the government
through the ballot box can affect policy outputs. This is political
power in its most obvious form. But the organization of interests
takes time and effort, and is most easily directed against threats to
one's well-being (Hansen 1985). While we can track through history
the organization of interests in terms of one group responding to the
mobilization of another, this is not a mechanical process (Walker
1983). Each specific mobilization requires effort and skill to
overcome the collective-action problem. The problems in the way
of some mobilizations means some groups are never effectively
organized. Other groups, smaller, richer, able to build coalitions
with groups already in the fray, more interactive and with the other
features we saw in Chapter 2 which enable mobilization, can
organize more easily. To use the analogy of a machine as in the
'anti-growth machine' is misleading. What makes the growth-
machine metaphor so powerful is the fact that the systematic luck of
developers and capital means that when they push development,
often they are pushing at an open door. The cards are stacked in
developers' favour. The structure of capitalist society makes
capitalists systematically lucky. The nature of the collective-action
problem also enables richer and smaller groups to mobilize more
easily, again enabling the production or growth side of any conflict
to have more power than the environmental or anti-growth side.
This does not mean that the anti-growth coalitions never win. Of
course they do. While larger numbers may mean that a group takes
longer to mobilize, larger numbers are also an advantage where
political leaders are democratically elected.

Regime theory

Regime theory is potentially a more general model of urban politics
than the growth and anti-growth models. In its original formu-
lations (Elkin 1987; Fainstein and Fainstein 1986; Stone 1989)
regime theory maps the close relationship between development

and urban politics; latterly it has developed into a broader account of the different array of politics to be found in American and European cities.

One of the defining features of Stone's (1989) account of Atlanta in regime terms is to explain how, despite changing personnel and ideology, the city's authorities continued to work closely with the business community. We explained this earlier as a result of the systematic luck of business whose interests are convergent or seen to be convergent with those of the governing politicians. Stone sees it as an example of 'systemic power' where the stratification of society constrains the possibilities of action for all groups in the case of governing coalitions by 'the impact of the larger socioeconomic system on the predispositions of public officials' (Stone 1980: 979, emphasis removed). In an analysis of four prominent mayors of US cities, Stone (1995) argues that they were individuals of extraordinary ability who used 'creative bounded choice' (Jones and Bachelor 1993) to rule. All four were involved in major developments in their cities; two managed to carry out somewhat redistributive policies, which may be thought to be against the interests of the business community. These regimes are all coalitions of electoral and monied interests man-oeuvring within constraints to remain in power and sustain their policies. Regimes develop, according to Stone, in order to deal with the complexity of urban politics and to create cooperation between disparate factions. Regimes are coordinating devices which provide opportunities for bargaining with the different sides in controversies and, importantly, establish the parameters of the bargaining game for all the participants. Regimes are defined by their purposes, and these provide the parameters through which bargaining takes place. Regime theory analyses urban politics through three factors: (1) the nature of the governing coalition; (2) the structure of relations between actors; and (3) the actors' resources. It is therefore a bargaining model of the urban political process.

Stone (1993) identifies four types of regime in American cities. Maintenance regimes seek to preserve the status quo. Their core task is to maintain routine service delivery. Development regimes seek to promote growth and halt the economic decline of parts of the city. Middle-class progressive regimes wish to manage growth and protect the environment – the so-called anti-growth machine.

The final category comprises regimes which require mass mobilization to expand the opportunities for the lower classes. Each regime
faces a collective-action problem, and the task of each governing
coalition is to match resources to the requirements of their
supporters. The difficulties of collective action may be thought to
deepen from the first to the fourth type of regime, though
stagnation in the first regime, unpopular development in the
second, reduced employment opportunities in the third may all
bring down regimes which fail to understand the expectations of
their constituency.

While regime theory concentrates upon the structure of relations
between actors, the resources they have and the manner in which
interests and preferences are shaped by the nature of society, it can
help us to understand the structure of power and luck in urban
communities. However, the danger for regime theory understood
very broadly, as for example by Savitch and Thomas (1991), is that
it becomes a description rather than an explanation of the different
types of politics which can exist in different communities (Stoker
1995). To label one community 'a maintenance regime' and another
a 'development regime' may describe the sorts of politics which
exist in two different communities. However, it does not itself
explain why one type of politics exists in one community and
another type in a second. For that we need to delve into the
production of interests and examine the nature of the resources and
the course of the bargaining game in each community.

Pluralism, elitism and state autonomy

The old debates in political science concerning the nature of the
state at both national and local level can now be seen in a deeper and
more compelling context. The pluralists have produced a welter of
case studies to show that at times, different groups, including the
disadvantaged, can get what they want. The 'who benefits test'
shows that even the disadvantaged can benefit by entering into the
political process. Given that the test of pluralism is not even that
stringent, Robert Dahl – the most famous pluralist of all – believes
that a polity can be described as pluralist if different groups can
bring costs to policy-makers (Dahl 1956, 1986). I do not even need
to persuade policy-makers to do what I want, as long as they have to
take my views into account. As long as they are forced to hear

'legitimate groups' and spend time and effort not doing what they ask, then we have a pluralist system.

Pluralists have also shown that different elites are involved in policy formation in different issue areas. This shows that it is not the same people getting what they want all the time, but rather different sets of people dominating in different policy arenas. Given that there are bound to be some who dominate, as long as it is not the same people, then we can say that we do not have a simple power elite in the manner C. Wright Mills (1956) suggested.

The breaking down of the policy-making structure into different issue areas has also been used by elite theorists to argue that an elite system does operate. Different issue areas are dominated by different sorts of 'policy network'. Some policy networks are highly contested and open, others are constrained and dominated by certain groups. These latter are usually called 'policy communities' (Dowding 1994, 1995). Elite theorists argue that policy communities are the norm and the most powerful groups include government agencies, and those groups which largely agree with government. This is the 'state autonomy' position. State autonomists argue that government by and large does what it wants. While it may appear in the pluralist case studies that numerous groups affect government policy, in fact groups only marginally modify what government wants to do, or create policy only where government is relatively indifferent. Where true conflict emerges, government usually gets its way. In fact, the way in which pluralists define pluralism and the difficulties of interpreting even simple case studies make it difficult to differentiate empirically between the two so-called rival theories (Christiansen and Dowding 1994).

It is clear that we will not understand the power structure merely by seeing who gets what and when; we need to understand why. Pluralists have tended to concentrate upon decisions which affect those groups whose organizations have in some way lobbied government at some level. However, other groups, both state actors and other interested groups, may have benefited without actually lobbying government. Furthermore, some groups may appear to have been successful in their lobbying – they may seem to be powerful; but if there was little resistance from government, then the group may have been pushing at an open door. We cannot study the power of groups by looking only at their resources; we also need to model the context in which decisions are taken, and consider the

	Lucky	Not Lucky
Powerful	1	2
Not Powerful	3	4

Figure 4.2 Power and luck.

resources of allies and putative rivals. The pluralists are correct that some groups play a major role in policy formation in many issue areas. But they are not correct in assuming that the welter of case studies showing that policy formation is complex with many winners and losers demonstrates the falsity of elitist arguments. They also need to show that groups get their way despite the resistance of state actors. Moreover, the plight of unorganized or under-mobilized groups cannot be ignored. It is not enough to show that there are a small number of elite actors involved in policy formation in most issue areas. We could not imagine the polity of a large nation in which policy is not formulated by a small minority of elites. The question is how far is policy organized in the interests of those elites, and how often are they forced through the pressure group system and the democratic process to keep their own self-interests at bay. Essentially, the debate between the rival positions can be seen in terms of the two-by-two matrix (see Figure 4.2).

Elitists claim that there are groups (which together make up a tiny minority of people) which fit in boxes 1 and 2 (usually in box 1) regarding the vast majority of issues, while most groups (constituting the vast majority of people) fit into boxes 3 and 4. There is a large degree of policy fit. Many people in the latter groups might agree with the policy outputs – they are in box 3. Many powerful people are lucky and so do not need to act to get the policy outcomes they desire – they are in box 1. The pluralist position as it is usually elucidated by its critics claims that all (or at least most) people are in all four boxes in different issue areas. A more realistic pluralist position (sometimes called neo-pluralism) can agree that some people might end up in box 4 more often than in box 1, and some in box 1 more often than in box 4, but must maintain that there is not a systematic bias and this does not occur for the vast majority of people over the most important issues. In other words, inequalities are dispersed, though there may be a small set of powerless and luckless people. An even weaker pluralist position (sometimes called reformed pluralism) maintains that while there may be some systematic bias, institutional structures exist which allow entry into box 2 for many people in different issue areas. That is, even if people do not always get what they want, if they feel strongly about some issue they can affect the policy process. The 'can' here is not simply some institutional right, but is also a real behavioural possibility. That is, the incentives against taking action are not so great that groups do not manage to mobilize and actually affect policy.

If most people are in box 3 most of the time, then they have little power but tend to get what they want. Such a situation is perfectly compatible with pluralist theory because pluralists maintain that organized groups will form only when their interests are threatened. Thus if one is lucky one does not need to be powerful. It is also compatible with elitist theory to the extent that most people might get what they want most of the time, but be unable to get what they want when they find that state and social structures act against their self-interests.

The approach to power which has been developed here allows us to get a handle on this debate. Pluralists claim that power in society is relatively diffuse, many groups are able to affect the policy process, and there is no single elite which dominates politics. Elitists hold that while many groups may at times affect the policy process, there are elites which do tend to dominate and get what they want. While there may be different sets of elites in different policy areas, some policy areas are more important than others. In urban politics, development issues are paramount, dominating politics in most communities and infecting other issues such as the environment, pollution, race, poverty and the provision of many services. Elite theorists believe that while different elites may operate in different issue areas, they tend to come from the same social class backgrounds. They argue that this dominance is not happenstance but can be explained by a causal mechanism, as we saw in Przeworski's argument and with the growth machine. We have seen that this makes sense, but that we cannot simply impute power to elites because they seem to benefit. Rather, they benefit through systematic luck. And it is the nature of systematic luck which makes it so hard to judge between the pluralist account of politics and the elite account. The heart of the debate is not, as is usually fondly imagined, empirical. It is normative. The question is not so much how often do certain groups tend to get what they want and others not get what they want. Rather, it is how often should we expect certain groups to benefit and others to fail. If the failure of many groups to achieve their aims is expected, then evidence that they sometimes succeed may suggest that they do have outcome power. If you are not surprised that developers tend to get their way, or that the interests of business as opposed to the interests of the homeless are more in the minds of policy-makers, the evidence that a poverty action group has managed to affect legislation will be taken as evidence of pluralism. However, if one's normative commitments are more egalitarian, then any evidence that benefits, or power, are not equally distributed will be taken as evidence of elitism.

We should no longer ask questions about how pluralist or elitist the state is. The fulcrum of comparison should be the openness and distribution of power in societies relative to how they have been in the past, to one another, and to how they could be. The last is more explicitly a normative question, which at least brings some of the real conflict between the different factions out into the open. The debate between elite theorists and pluralists is largely a normative one cowering in empirical disguise. To begin by asking the last question and bringing into play evidence drawn from the answers to the earlier questions would be honest, if no less fraught with difficulties.

Normative questions

The power to do great good is also the power to do great evil. We may wish to empower individuals to live their lives as they see fit, and to empower collectivities, for people working together have far more power to get the outcomes they want than individuals can ever have on their own. How individuals and groups use the power they have is another matter. While the desire to empower people may be genuine, we still want limits on that power. Egalitarians may wish to see much greater equality of outcome power, though they may also wish to see unequal distributions of social power, with social power in the hands of democratically constrained institutions.

How far power should be equalized depends upon how far it can be equalized. 'Ought' implies 'can'. It also depends upon one's views on a whole host of other normative issues. Power and freedom are closely related concepts but they are not equivalent. Individuals may be free to do something which they do not have the power to do, or they may perform actions which they are not free to do. Liberty is not the same as ability. When we talk of legal freedom we are speaking of what we may legally do without sanction from the state. The conscientious objector has the outcome power to refuse to fight but is not free not to fight. Incentives are created to try to make conscientious objectors fight: they may face ridicule or threats from their friends and neighbours, and the state may threaten them with gaol. In this way, by carefully specifying scope modifiers, outcome power and freedom may seem equivalent, as the 'physicalist' approach to liberty at times seems to make them (Steiner 1994). However, we cannot claim that we are free to do everything we can do, because collective action allows us to do everything physically and technically possible while, conversely, without collective action individually we can do none of the things we daily take for granted. Legal freedom may be easy to specify, social freedom less so, for it is affected by the sorts of incentives that actors other than the state set up.

The power debate is essentially normative because of the relationship between power and freedom, which leads to questions about the rights and distribution of property. Those who feel that existing property rights are justified, or who think that, even if they are not, empirical political scientists should not comment on this in their work, may believe that modern industrial democracies are pluralist because power is distributed as widely as can be expected. We may believe that the systematic luck of capital under capitalism is right and proper, indeed needs to be encouraged. To the extent that the wealth of nations is based upon their degree of development, anything which adds to growth opportunities enhances the wealth of the nation. Business should not have to fight for growth potential since growth is good for virtually everyone, and if some gain more than others then that is all that can be expected.

Elitists discover that some groups get what they want more often than others through luck and through power. They discover mechanisms by which those who gain do so systematically. They believe that these mechanisms do not have to operate in these ways, and luck and outcome power may be more equally distributed. By demonstrating that some groups gain more often than others, and gain at the expense of others, elitists hope to persuade us that society needs to be changed. The distribution of wealth brought about by growth can be used in ways which benefit more people.

The realization that growth does not always help local communities but rather benefits outsiders may help overcome the systematic luck of developers. Elitists believe that by uncovering the processes of government we may be able to see better ways of running government in more equitable and socially just ways.

The fact that different writers can study the same processes and reach different conclusions about the distribution of power does not mean that there is no point in empirically studying power, simply that what is discovered will be open to different interpretations given prior normative stances. The political scientist must simply be prepared to engage in justification of his or her moral stance with regard to some of the important empirical questions of the day. All empirical matters are subject to theoretical interpretation and moral questioning, but this does not make them any less empirical. It just means that we need to carefully justify our approach to studying the world and understand the importance our studies have for the conclusions we draw about the way in which we wish to govern ourselves.

References

Axelrod, R. (1984) *The Evolution of Cooperation*. New York: Basic Books.

Barry, B. (1978) *Sociologists, Economists and Democracy*, 2nd edn. Chicago, IL: University of Chicago Press.

Barry, B. (1988) 'Review article: Uses of "power"', *Government and Opposition*, **23**, 340–53.

Barry, B. (1991) 'Is it better to be powerful or lucky?', in *Democracy and Power*. Oxford: Clarendon Press.

Barry, B. and Rae, D. (1975) 'Political evaluation', in D. Greenstein and N. Polsby (eds) *Political Science: Scope and Theory*. Handbook of Political Science, Vol. 1. Reading, MA: Addison-Wesley.

Beetham, D. (1985) *Max Weber and the Theory of Modern Politics*. Cambridge: Polity Press.

Berkeley, G. (1962) *The Principles of Human Knowledge*. Glasgow: Fontana (first published 1710).

Bianco, W. T. and Tsebelis, G. (1990) 'Crime and punishment: Are one-shot two-person games enough?', *American Political Science Review*, **84**, 569–86.

Brams, S. J. (1990) *Negotiation Games: Applying Game Theory to Bargaining and Arbitration*. New York: Routledge.

Brams, S. J. (1994) *Theory of Moves*. Cambridge: Cambridge University Press.

Carling, A. (1991) *Social Division*. London: Verso.

Caro, R. (1974) *The Power Broker*. New York: Alfred A. Knopf.

Chong, D. (1991) *Collective Action and the Civil Rights Movement*. Chicago, IL: University of Chicago Press.

Christiansen, L. and Dowding, K. (1994) 'Pluralism or state autonomy? The case of Amnesty International (British Section): The insider/ outsider group', *Political Studies*, **42**, 15–24.

Clark, T. N. and Fergusen, L. C. (1983) *City Money: Political Processes,*

Fiscal Strain, and Retrenchment. New York: Columbia University Press.

Clark, T. N. and Goetz, E. (1994) 'The antigrowth machine: Can city governments control, limit or manage growth?', in T. N. Clark (ed.) *Urban Innovation: Creative Strategies for Turbulent Times.* London: Sage.

Coates, D. (1984) *The Context of British Politics.* London: Hutchinson.

Cox, K. R. and Mair, A. (1989) 'Urban growth machines and the politics of local economic development', *International Journal for Urban and Regional Research,* **13,** 137–46.

Crenson, M. (1971) *The Unpolitics of Air Pollution.* Baltimore, MA: Johns Hopkins University Press.

Dahl, R. A. (1956) *A Preface to Democratic Theory.* Chicago, IL: University of Chicago Press.

Dahl, R. A. (1968) 'Power', in D. L. Sils (ed.) *International Encylopedia of the Social Sciences,* Vol. 12. New York: Free Press.

Dahl, R. A. (1986) 'Rethinking *Who Governs?*: New Haven Revisited' in R. Waste (ed.) *Community Power: Directions for Future Research.* Beverly Hills, CA: Sage.

Denzin, N. K. (1978) *The Research Act: A Theoretical Introduction to Sociological Methods,* 2nd edn. New York: McGraw-Hill.

Domhoff, G. W. (1983) *Who Rules America Now?* Englewood Cliffs, NJ: Prentice-Hall.

Domhoff, G. W. (1986) 'The growth regime and the power elite', in R. Waste (ed.) *Community Power: Directions for Future Research.* Beverly Hills, CA: Sage.

Dowding, K. (1991) *Rational Choice and Political Power.* Aldershot: Edward Elgar.

Dowding, K. (1992) 'Choice: Its increase and its value', *British Journal of Political Science,* **22,** 301–14.

Dowding, K. (1994) 'Policy communities: Don't stretch a good idea too far', in P. J. Dunleavy and J. Stanyer (eds) *Contemporary Political Studies, 1994,* Vol. 1. Belfast: Political Studies Association.

Dowding, K. (1995) 'Model or metaphor? A critical review of the policy network approach', *Political Studies,* **43,** 136–58.

Dowding, K. and Dunleavy, P. (in press) 'Production, disbursement and consumption: The modes and modalities of goods and services', *Sociological Review.*

Downs, A. (1957) *An Economic Theory of Democracy.* New York: Harper and Row.

Dunleavy, P. (1991) *Democracy, Bureaucracy and Public Choice.* Hemel Hempstead: Harvester.

Elkin, S. (1987) *City and Regime in the American Republic.* Chicago, IL: University of Chicago Press.

Ellis, W. (1995) *The Oxbridge Conspiracy*. Harmondsworth: Penguin.

Elster, J. (1988) 'Marx, revolution and rational choice', in M. Taylor (ed.) *Rationality and Revolution*. Cambridge: Cambridge University Press.

Fainstein, N. and Fainstein, S. (1986) 'Regime Strategies, Communal Resistance and Economic Forces', in S. Fainstein, R. C. Hill, D. Judd and M. Smith (eds) *Restructuring the City: The Political Economy of Urban Redevelopment*. New York: Longman.

Foucault, M. (1980) *Power/Knowledge: Selected Interviews and Other Writings 1972–1977* (edited by C. Gordon). Brighton: Harvester.

Friedman, R. (1973) 'On the concept of authority in political philosophy', in R. E. Flathman (ed.) *Concepts in Social and Political Philosophy*. New York: Macmillan.

Friedrich, C. (1941) *Constitutional Government and Democracy*. New York: W. W. Norton.

Frohlich, N. and Oppenheimer, J. (1970) 'I get by with a little help from my friends', *World Politics,* **23**, 104–20.

Frohlich, N., Oppenheimer, J. and Young, O. (1971) *Political Leadership and Collective Goods*. Princeton, NJ: Princeton University Press.

Fudenberg, D. and Tirole, J. (1991) *Game Theory*. Cambridge, MA: The MIT Press.

Gambetta, D. (1993) *The Sicilian Mafia: The Business of Private Protection*. Cambridge, MA: Harvard University Press.

Gaventa, J. (1980) *Power and Powerlessness: Quiescence and Rebellion in an Appalachian Valley*. Oxford: Clarendon Press.

Grant, W. (1987) *Business and Politics in Britain*. London: Macmillan.

Green, L. (1988) *The Authority of the State*. Oxford: Clarendon Press.

Hansen, J. N. (1985) 'The political economy of group membership', *American Political Science Review,* **79**, 79–96.

Hardin, R. (1982) *Collective Action*. Baltimore, MD: Resources for the Future.

Harding, A. (1991) 'The rise of urban growth coalitions, UK-style?', *Government and Policy,* **9**, 295–317.

Harding, A. (1994) 'Urban regimes and growth machines: Towards a cross-national research agenda', *Urban Affairs Quarterly,* **29**, 356–82.

Harding, A. (1995) 'Elite theory and growth machines', in D. Judge, G. Stoker and H. Wolman (eds) *Theories of Urban Politics*. London: Sage.

Harsanyi, J. C. (1976a) 'Measurement of social power, opportunity costs, and the theory of two-person bargaining games', in *Essays on Ethics, Social Behaviour and Scientific Explanation*. Dordrecht: Reidel.

Harsanyi, J. C. (1976b) 'Measurement of social power in *n*-person reciprocal power situations', in *Essays on Ethics, Social Behaviour and Scientific Explanation*. Dordrecht: Reidel.

Hart, H. L. A. (1982) *Essays on Bentham*. Oxford: Clarendon Press.

Heap, S. H. and Varoufakis, Y. (1995) *Game Theory: A Critical Introduction*. London: Routledge.

Heinz, J. P., Laumann, E. O., Nelson, R. L. and Salisbury, R. H. (1993) *The Hollow Core: Private Interests in National Policy Making*. Cambridge, MA: Harvard University Press.

Hirschman, A. O. (1983) *Shifting Involvements*. Oxford: Martin Robertson.

Horan, C. (1991) 'Beyond governing coalitions: Analyzing urban regimes in the 1990s', *Journal of Urban Affairs*, **13**, 119–35.

Hume, D. (1975) *Enquiries Concerning Human Understanding and Concerning the Principles of Morals*, 3rd edn (revised by P. H. Nidditch). Oxford: Oxford University Press (first published 1772).

Hunter, F. (1963) *Community Power Structure: A Study of Decision Makers*. New York: Anchor Books (first published 1953).

Hutton, W. (1996) *The State We're In*. London: Vintage.

Jick, T. D. (1979) 'Mixing qualitative and quantitative methods: Triangulation in action', *Administrative Science Quarterly*, **24**, 602–61.

Jones, B. and Bachelor, L. (1993) *The Sustaining Hand: Community Leadership and Corporate Power*, 2nd edn (revised). Lawrence, KS: University of Kansas Press.

Jordan, A. G. and Richardson, J. J. (1987a) *Government and Pressure Groups in Britain*. Oxford: Clarendon Press.

Jordan, A. G. and Richardson, J. J. (1987b) *British Politics and the Policy Process*. London: Unwin Hyman.

Kimber, R. (1993) 'Interest groups and the fallacy of the liberal fallacy', in J. J. Richardson (ed.) *Pressure Groups*. Oxford: Oxford University Press.

Laswell, H. (1936) *Who Gets What, When and How*. New York: Whittlesey House.

Lindblom, C. E. (1977) *Politics and Markets*. New York: Basic Books.

Logan, J. and Molotch, H. (1984) 'Tensions in the growth machine: Overcoming resistance to value-free development', *Social Problems*, **31**, 483–99.

Logan, J. and Molotch, H. (1987) *Urban Fortunes: The Political Economy of Place*. Berkeley, CA: University of California Press.

Marsh, D. (1976) 'On joining interest groups: An empirical consideration of the work of Mancur Olson Jr.', *British Journal of Political Science*, **6**, 257–71.

Marsh, D. and Rhodes, R. A. W. (eds) (1992) *Policy Networks in British Government*. Oxford: Oxford University Press.

Marwell, G. and Oliver, P. (1993) *The Critical Mass in Collective Action*. Cambridge: Cambridge University Press.

Mills, C. W. (1956) *The Power Elite*. New York: Oxford University Press.

Moe, T. M. (1980) *The Organization of Interests*. Chicago, IL: University of Chicago Press.

Molotch, H. (1976) 'The city as a growth machine', *American Journal of Sociology'*, **82**, 309–55.

Molotch, H. (1979) 'Capital and neighborhood in the United States', *Urban Affairs Quarterly*, **14**, 289–312.

Molotch, H. (1990) 'Urban deals in comparative perspective', in J. Logan and T. Swanstrom (eds) *Beyond the City Limits: Urban Policy and Economic Restructuring in Comparative Perspective*. Philadelphia, PA: Temple University Press.

Molotch, H. and Logan, J. (1990) 'The space for urban action: Urban fortunes. A rejoinder', *Political Geography Quarterly*, **9**, 85–92.

Molotch, H. and Vicari, S. (1988) 'Three ways to build: The development process in the US, Japan and Italy', *Urban Affairs Quarterly*, **24**, 188–214.

Morriss, P. (1987) *Power: A Philosophical Analysis*. Manchester: Manchester University Press.

Morrow, J. D. (1994) *Game Theory for Political Scientists*. Princeton, NJ: Princeton University Press.

Nagel, J. (1975) *The Descriptive Analysis of Power*. New Haven, CT: Yale University Press.

Oliver, P. (1984) 'If you don't do it, nobody else will: Active and token contributors to local collective action', *American Sociological Review*, **49**, 601–10.

Olson, M. (1971) *The Logic of Collective Action*, 2nd edn. Cambridge, MA: Harvard University Press.

Olson, M. (1982) *The Rise and Decline of Nations*. New Haven, CT: Yale University Press.

Ordeshook, P. C. (1986) *Game Theory and Political Theory*. Cambridge: Cambridge University Press.

Ordeshook, P. C. (1992) *A Political Theory Primer*. London: Routledge.

Orr, M. and Stoker, G. (1994) 'Urban regimes and leadership in Detroit', *Urban Affairs Quarterly*, **30**, 48–73.

Petracca, M. P. (ed.) (1992) *The Politics of Interests: Interest Groups Transformed*. Boulder, CO: Westview Press.

Popper, K. (1957) *The Poverty of Historicism*. London: Routledge & Kegan Paul.

Przeworski, A. (1986) *Capitalism and Social Democracy*. Cambridge: Cambridge University Press.

Przeworski, A. and Sprague, J. (1985) *Paper Stones: A History of Electoral Socialism*. Chicago, IL: University of Chicago Press.

Rasmusen, E. (1989) *Games and Information: An Introduction to Game Theory*. Oxford: Blackwell.

Raz, J. (1986) *The Morality of Freedom*. Oxford: Clarendon Press.

Rescher, N. (1975) *A Theory of Possibility*. Oxford: Oxford University Press.

Rhodes, R. A. W. (1988) *Beyond Westminster and Whitehall*. London: Unwin Hyman.

Rhodes, R. A. W. and Marsh, D. (eds) (1992) *Policy Networks in British Government*. Oxford: Oxford University Press.

Riker, W. H. (1982) *Liberalism Against Populism*. San Francisco, CA: W. H. Freeman & Co.

Sabatier, P. and Jenkins-Smith, H. C. (eds) (1993) *Policy Change and Learning: An Advocacy Coalition Approach*. Boulder, CO: Westview Press.

Samuelson, P. A. (1954) 'The pure theory of public expenditure', *Review of Economics and Statistics*, **36**, 387–9.

Samuelson, P. A. (1955) 'Diagrammatic exposition of a theory of public expenditure', *Review of Economics and Statistics*, **37**, 350–6.

Sandler, T. (1992) *Collective Action: Theory and Applications*. Ann Arbor, MI: University of Michigan Press.

Sartre, J.-P. (1949) *Iron in the Soul*. Harmondsworth: Penguin.

Savitch, H. and Thomas, J. (1991) 'Conclusion: End of the millennium in big city politics', in H. Savitch and J. Thomas (eds) *Big City Politics in Transition*. Newbury Park, CA: Sage.

Schelling, T. (1966) *Arms and Influence*. New Haven, CT: Yale University Press.

Schick, F. (1982) 'Under which descriptions?', in A. Sen and B. Williams (eds) *Utilitarianism and Beyond*. Cambridge: Cambridge University Press.

Schneider, M., Teske, P. and Mintrom, M. (1995) *Public Entrepreneurs: Agents for Change in American Government*. Princeton, NJ: Princeton University Press.

Schondhart-Bailey, C. and Bailey, A. (1995) 'The buck in your bank is not a vote for free trade: Financial intermediation and trade preferences in the United States and Germany', in K. Dowding and D. King (eds) *Preferences, Institutions, and Rational Choice*. Oxford: Clarendon Press.

Segal, J. A. and Cover, A. A. (1989) 'Ideological values and the votes of U.S. Supreme Court Justices', *American Political Science Review*, **83**, 557–65.

Shapley, L. S. (1967) 'On committees', in F. Zwicky and A.G. Wilson (eds) *New Methods of Thoughts and Procedure*. New York: Springer-Verlag.

Shapley, L. S. (1981) 'Measurement of power in political systems', *Proceedings of Symposia in Applied Mathematics*, **24**, 69–81.

Shapley, L. S. and Shubik, M. (1969) 'A method for evaluating the distribution of power in a committee system', in R. Bell, D. V. Edwards and R. H. Wagner (eds) *Political Power: A Reader*. London: Collier-Macmillan.

Simon, H. A. (1969) 'Notes on the observation and measurement of power', in R. Bell, D. V. Edwards and R. H. Wagner (eds) *Political Power: A Reader*. London: Collier-Macmillan.

Steinbeck, J. (1939) *The Grapes of Wrath*. Harmondsworth: Penguin.

Steiner, H. (1994) *An Essay on Rights*. Oxford: Blackwell.

Stoker, G. (1995) 'Regime theory and urban politics', in D. Judge, G. Stoker and H. Wolman (eds) *Theories of Urban Politics*. London: Sage.

Stoker, G. and Mossberger, K. (1994) 'Urban regime theory in comparative perspective', *Government and Policy*, **12**, 195–212.

Stone, C. (1980) 'Systemic power in community decision making: A restatement of stratification theory', *American Political Science Review*, **74**, 978–90.

Stone, C. (1987a) 'The study of the politics of urban developments', in C. Stone and H. T. Sanders (eds) *The Politics of Urban Development*. Lawrence, KS: University of Kansas Press.

Stone, C. (1987b) 'Elite distemper versus the promise of democracy', in G. W. Domhoff and T. R. Dye (eds) *Power Elites and Organizations*. Beverly Hills, CA: Sage.

Stone, C. (1989) *Regime Politics: Governing Atlanta 1946–1988*. Lawrence, KS: University of Kansas Press.

Stone, C. (1993) 'Urban regimes and the capacity to govern: A political economy approach', *Journal of Urban Affairs*, **15**, 1–28.

Stone, C. (1995) 'Political leadership and urban politics', in D. Judge, G. Stoker and H. Wolman (eds) *Theories of Urban Politics*. London: Sage.

Tannahill, R. (1975) *Food in History*. St Albans: Paladin.

Taylor, M. (1987) *The Possibility of Cooperation*. Cambridge: Cambridge University Press.

Truman, D. (1951) *The Governmental Process*. New York: Alfred A. Knopf.

Tsebelis, G. (1990) 'Penalty has no impact on crime: A game theoretical analysis', *Rationality and Society*, **2**, 255–86.

Tsebelis, G. (1991) 'The effect of fines on regulated industries: Game theory *vs* decision theory', *Journal of Theoretical Politics*, **3**, 81–101.

Walker, J. (1983) 'The origin and maintenance of interest groups in America', *American Political Science Review*, **77**, 390–406.

Ward, H. (1987a) 'The risks of a reputation for toughness: Strategy in public goods provision problems modelled by Chicken super-games', *British Journal of Political Science*, **17**, 23–52.

Ward, H. (1987b) 'Structural power – a contradiction in terms?', *Political Studies*, **35**, 593–610.

Ward, H. (1989) 'Testing the waters: Taking risks to gain reassurance in public goods games', *Journal of Conflict Resolution*, **33**, 274–308.

Weber, M. (1978) *Economy and Society*, Vols 1 and 2 (edited by G. Roth and C. Wittich). Berkeley, CA: University of California Press.

White, A. (1975) *Modal Thinking*. Oxford: Blackwell.

Winner, L. (1980) 'Do artifacts have politics?', *Daedelus*, Winter, pp. 121–36.

Index